PEACE, VALUE, AND WISDOM

The Educational Philosophy of Daisaku Ikeda

VIBS

Volume 122

A volume in **Daisaku Ikeda Studies**
DIS
George David Miller, Editor

Cover design: Gregory Harms (FARMHOUSE/ga)

The paper on which this book is printed meets the requirements of "ISO 9706:1994, Information and documentation - Paper for documents - Requirements for permanence".

ISBN: 90-420-1359-1

Printed in The Netherlands

PEACE, VALUE, AND WISDOM

The Educational Philosophy of Daisaku Ikeda

George David Miller

Amsterdam – New York, NY 2002

CONTENTS

LIST OF ILLUSTRATIONS

Photographs

FOREWORD

In the following pages, George David Miller offers a rigorous treatment of the educational philosophy of Daisaku Ikeda. Traversing the broad borders and unearthing the rich content of Ikeda's cosmic humanistic philosophy, the book examines vital issues such as the spirituality of wisdom, the integration of compassion and intellect, inner revolution, cosmic citizenship, peace and cooperation, self-esteem, violence, nihilism, and apathy. Miller's account is bright and pithy, tracing the Buddhist and twentieth-century humanistic roots of Ikeda's philosophy and illustrating how Ikeda's notion of human or inner revolution is applicable to the vital contemporary concerns of educators.

One of the most vital concerns of educators in democratic societies is how students can become active participants in the democratic process. On July 4, 1776, the Declaration of Independence of the United States of America became a reality with this pronouncement: "We hold these truths to be self-evident, that all men [and women] are created equal, that they are endowed by their Creator with certain unalienable Rights, that among these are Life, Liberty, and the pursuit of Happiness."

When the founding fathers of the United States of America penned these words 225 years ago, they pointed the world in the direction of democracy and inclusiveness. Since then, there have been those among us who keep bringing us back to the grand and noble idea of democracy.

Mohandas Karamchand "Mahatma" Gandhi once said: "Civilization is the encouragement of differences. Civilization thus becomes a synonym of democracy. Force, violence, pressure, or compulsion with a view to conformity is, therefore, both uncivilized and undemocratic." The Reverend Dr. Martin Luther King, Jr., the leader of the Civil Rights Movement in the United States, also understood the deep well of democracy and wanted the world house to drink from that well. King said:

> We have inherited a large house, a great 'world house' in which we have to live together—black and white, Easterner and Westerner, Gentile and Jew, Catholic and Protestant, Moslem and Hindu, [Buddhist and Bedouin]—a family unduly separated in ideas, culture and interest, who because we can never again live apart, must learn somehow to live with each other in peace.[1]

How do we learn to live in peace? How do we learn to live the lessons of democracy? Thomas Jefferson said democracy cannot survive with an ignorant population. For centuries, we have depended on our institutions of higher education to teach us community, humanity, service, and happiness. W. E. B.

DuBois once remarked:

> The function of the university is not simply to teach breadwinning, or to furnish teachers for the public schools or to be a centre of polite society. It is, above all, to be the organ of that fine adjustment between real life and the growing knowledge of life, an adjustment which forms the secret of civilization.[2]

And so for the sake of democracy envisioned by our forefathers; for the sake of civilization as conceived by Gandhi; and for the sake of civil rights imagined by King, we need new educational institutions to teach us Daisaku Ikeda's civility for the uplift of all human personality and the environment. Ikeda's philosophy of education can help us grow up into democracy's crown. Ikeda's educational theory is founded on the use of the power of education to promote respect and peaceful coexistence around the world.

Today, more than ever, we need a certain kind of educational institution that promotes international exchange, cross-cultural dialogue, and environmental justice for all of us to blossom and self-actualize to the maximum. Benjamin Elijah Mays, Martin Luther King, Jr., Mohandas Karamchand Gandhi, and Daisaku Ikeda all had extensive international, interracial, interdisciplinary, and interreligious educations through a worldwide dialogue. All of this dialogue has the goal of freedom, liberty, equality, equity, coherently critical thinking, ecological responsibility, peace, nonviolence, happiness, value creation, and the building of a new world humanitarian order. This change has the goal of inclusive democracy.

Some of the language today which points to the moral frontiers of this profound change in our evolving democracy for the next century includes: civility, diversity maturity, the vertically challenged, gender justice, global excellence, quality control, integrity, the physically challenged, gender-neutral, inclusive language, sustainability, religious pluralism, multiculturalism, cloning, communication between silos, universal human, smoke free zones, profanity free zones, homophobia, distance learning, issue sensitive, time sensitive, quantum leap, xenophobia, and value creation.

The American Civil and Human Rights Nonviolent Movement was a time of open struggle for international democracy, and uniting our divided world house. In this Movement, we rehearsed for the democracy that is to be. The Civil Rights Movement turned the stupid, stumbling South into the sunshine states because, "A moral person cannot patiently adjust to injustice." That is where Gandhi, King, and Ikeda are different. They have all taught the necessity of inclusiveness.

The cause of Civil Rights, which began as a point of entry for excluded minorities into the larger society, helped revitalize the American

Democratic ethos, as Martin Luther King, Jr. had intended. That rehearsal time broke down barriers for women all over the world. The notion of men being leaders and women backing us up is not in the spirit of democracy. Women and men should work side by side on the front lines—women are also leaders. Women in Montgomery, Alabama, for example, stayed up overnight and printed 35,000 flyers outlining what happened to Rosa Parks.

We certainly have enjoyed much progress since the Civil Rights Movement. Today, our challenge and our responsibility are to grow into the crown of our possibilities. We must grow into the crowns of civilization, civil right, and civility. We must grow into the crown of democracy. We must be the change we wish to see, as Gandhi challenges us.

Through his educational philosophy, Ikeda has placed a crown of civility above the heads of global citizens with the hope we will grow tall enough to wear it. "Education must foster love for humanity, develop character, and provide an intellectual foundation for realizing peace and empowering people to contribute to society."

Ikeda emphasizes an education that calls for a revolution of the inner life. A human revolution that does not confuse knowledge for wisdom, but develops compassionate wisdom, by focusing on the deepest and most universal dimensions of life, resulting in a natural empathy toward life in its infinite diversity. The failure of empathy makes violence possible. Our goal as "spiritual beings, planetary citizens, and human incarnations" must be diversity/maturity. We arrive at this global end by using the methods of what Ikeda calls "soft power," dialogue, and cooperation.

We have in the twentieth century a near triumph of liberal democracy. Vincent Harding helps us ask some relevant questions: How do we expand democracy in the poorest communities in this country? What is democratic economics, democratic health care, democratic distribution of the wealth? Where are the centers for democracy? How shall American democracy be redeveloped and expanded? How do we achieve the political and spiritual deepening of democracy into education, religion, science and the arts? How do we create a multi-racial and international democracy? What kind of democratic practice will give the world peace? America is still a developing nation, maybe even ethically a third world nation when you consider how frightened we are of differences that we have created.

By happiness, Daisaku Ikeda, like Tsunesaburo Makiguchi and Josei Toda, does not mean mere pleasure, indulgence, self-seeking, cowardice, indolence, or complacency where the development of personality ceases. From these egoistic perspectives, we are left with immature and arrogant individuals, unable to grow out of their childish ways of never listening to others. Ikeda talks about an attitude of creativity, exhilaration, joy, accomplishment, deep fulfillment, purpose, and enlightenment that evokes creativity in students.

Happiness is obtained through fully realizing our potential, while not being swayed by circumstances, but seeking to tower above misfortune.

Freedom is a constant creation of value. Freedom is not a gift. It is an achievement. If our dreams for democracy are to be actualized, every citizen in our nation is going to have to be educated to the limit of his or her capacity. And I don't mean accommodated, adjusted, amused, exercised, or trained. Ikeda's proactive educational philosophy of hope inspires us to hold freedom seminars around the many meanings of freedom, and also institutionalize intergenerational seminars and conversations about new careers on how to live together peacefully across racial lines, as well as how to save the environment.

Freedom has a purpose. Freedom is for the pursuit of happiness and service. It is for the development of the individual and of society. Freedom gives us the release from the great burden of uniformity, and releases value creation. If two people agree on everything all the time, says Vincent Harding, then one of them is unnecessary. It is only when we are in dialogue that we are most human. There is something special about multi-lateral dialogue, one in which we are all minorities.

We are citizens of a world that does not yet fully exist. The future is an infinite succession of present moments. We must learn to live together now what we believe to be the best of the ideals we treasure. We must abandon anti-democratic and uncivil practices. Daisaku Ikeda holds a crown above our heads with the hope that we will grow tall enough to wear it. He encourages us in Gandhi's words to "be the change we wish to see."

And when we have grown up into democracy's crown, we will have answered the anguished echo from all of the wisest humane reformers: Roger Williams's call for religious liberty; Samuel Adams's call for political liberty; Henry David Thoreau's denunciation of coercion; William Lloyd Garrison's demand for emancipation; Eugene V. Debs's cry for economic equality; Robert Maynard Hutchins's insistence that democracy requires liberal education for all; Martin Luther King, Jr.'s dream to be judged by the content of one's character and not by the color of one's skin; Nichiren Daishonin's call for perceiving the Mystic Truth inherent in all living beings; and Daisaku Ikeda's challenge that we be the highest seat of learning for humanity, the cradle of a new culture, and a fortress for the peace of humankind.

Then we will be able to live together in a great world house in peace, respecting the worth and dignity of all human personality as sacred. This is the *raison d'être* for Ikeda's educational philosophy and the institutional embodiment of it (most recently in Soka University of America), as we attempt to wear democracy's crown in a new century and millennium that will emphasize the greatest ideals of democracy—civilization, civil rights and civility—when the grand idea of democracy envisioned in the Declaration of Independence blooms for everybody around the globe.

In *Peace, Value, and Wisdom*, George David Miller illustrates what a perfect fit Ikeda's educational philosophy is for democracy's crown.

Democracy flourishes only when the populace is enlightened, can dialogue and cooperate in spite of differences, and build a society of hope pointing toward the ultimate goal of peaceful co-existence. Ikeda's philosophy of education can be an indispensable tool for educators on all levels to begin molding our spirits and public policies to fit into that crown.

Lawrence Edward Carter, Sr.
Dean, Martin Luther King, Jr.
International Chapel
Morehouse College

ACKNOWLEDGEMENTS

I never imagined writing a book of this sort. I never imagined writing an article, much less a book, on the pedagogical theories of a Japanese philosopher. Continental philosophy, the ethics of caring, and Freirean pedagogy have been my tofu and potatoes. Yet sometimes things just compel you to write. And this was one of those times.

I could not have written this book without the wonderful support of many people.

Daisaku Ikeda—thank you for your gracious hospitality in Japan in September 2000. I have never felt more welcomed anywhere in the world. You undoubtedly wrote the gospel on hospitality and graciousness. Thank you for inspiring me and helping me see the world differently. The following poem—"Bearers of Light," which I wrote on the plane coming home from Japan—is dedicated to your exploits:

bearers of light
like you, me, and Prometheus
are deemed arsonists
by fire departments
devoted to extinguishing truth

these fire departments
would rather us raze
their villages to cinder
than enlighten just one soul

because they see
that our light
starts soul fires
conscientious conflagrations

they have placed fire extinguishers
at every corner
waiting to put out fires
which they always imagine
to be furious forest fires

I admit I'm a pyromaniac
when it comes to lighting fires
in other people's hearts and minds
I love to watch from a distance
as their eyes light up

and their souls burn with life

Lawrence Edward Carter, Sr.—thank you for opening the door to Japan for me and giving me the opportunity to become familiar with Soka Gakkai International (SGI) and the educational philosophy of Daisaku Ikeda. We have been through a lot in these past years, and if ever two people had a symbiotic relationship, it's you and me.

To the great people at SGI—my sincere thanks. You made my job so much easier by bequeathing me a small library of Daisaku Ikeda's works in English, including dialogues, photography books, poetry, journal articles, and children's books. Special thanks to Danny Nagashima, Ian McIlraith, and Guy McCloskey. Danny, who was with me every step of the way in Japan, has been a delight and a good, solid friend. I am appreciative that you have championed my cause on so many occasions. Ian has done much to make the path easier for me. Guy sent me a steady stream of Daisaku Ikeda's books, articles, and addresses, which proved extremely useful. He offered judicious counsel at every turn. Thanks, too, to Lisa Kirk for your help during the final stages of this venture.

My wife, Norma, backs me up on everything I do and this book is no different. Once again, your photographic genius made a philosopher's face look acceptable on the back cover. Hon, I promise to thatch the yard more often next year. Laura and Anna, my daughters, have been patient with me as we split time on the computer. During those sometimes tense times, we didn't achieve *kōsen-rufu*, but we did manage to make it work out. You're all wonderful, and I am blessed that you are around every day.

Mark Roelof Eleveld, the author the Epilogue, has been a supportive friend when the foundations of my existence shook. He is friend with a capital F.

Ron Maruszak lent his eagle eyes to proofreading the manuscript, and his critique helped tighten the text.

Angli Sandhir offered keen suggestions that strengthened this work.

To Robert Ginsberg, who has supported me in every creative philosophical effort for the last decade, I am full of gratitude. Thanks for all the opportunities and for allowing me to express myself in nontraditional ways.

Grateful acknowledgement is made to the Soka Gakkai International-USA for resources and references, including quotations of passages from books and poems by Daisaku Ikeda and photographs used in this volume.

Grateful acknowledgement is also made to EM Press for permission to quote from *Storms Beneath the Skin* by Regie Gibson and *Children of Kosen-Rufu* by George David Miller.

INTRODUCTION

1. The Life Work of Daisaku Ikeda: Peace Through Education

The life work of Daisaku Ikeda rivals the feats of many of the twentieth century Nobel Prize winners.

Several of the laureates of the 1990s have been recognized for their achievements in volatile regions of the world: Kim Dae Jung for his work for human rights and democracy South Korea; John Hume and David Trimble for their efforts in Northern Ireland; and Yassar Arafat, Shimon Peres, and Yitzhak Rabin in the Middle East. Daisaku Ikeda has used the power of education to promote peace in the most volatile area of all: the human soul.

The six peace and cultural institutions, 1,000 cultural centers, and 13 educational institutions (kindergartens, elementary schools, junior and senior high schools, and universities) he has founded in Japan and abroad are deeply entrenched in the philosophy of peace through education. The motto of Soka University of Japan is:

> Be the Highest Seat of Learning for Humanity
> Be the Cradle of a New Culture
> Be a Fortress for the Peace of Humankind

As president of Soka Gakkai International, a global association of over 12 million lay Buddhists worldwide, Daisaku Ikeda promotes a philosophy based on respect and peaceful co-existence. Under his leadership, membership in Soka Gakkei has risen from 750,00 to over 12 million. The peace that Ikeda advocates is not simply a peace between people, but a comprehensive peace including inner peace and peace with the environment. Like Desmond Tutu and Nelson Mandela, Daisaku Ikeda fights oppression. For Ikeda, the enlightenment and liberation of the human soul is a prerequisite for eliminating oppression and building a peaceful world community in which all people can flourish.

In some sense, Ikeda is doing the same kind of work on the spiritual level that the International Campaign to Ban Landmines and Jody Williams (1997) did out in the field: instead of banning and clearing of anti-personnel mines, Ikeda has devoted his life work to clearing the "inner" land mines preventing humanity from achieving peaceful co-existence. In the same way the Red Cross, UNICEF, and Amnesty International seek to mitigate physical suffering, Ikeda seeks to end the spiritual suffering, which he believes is the basis for social ills. He calls for a human revolution in each person. Whereas Doctors Without Borders provide medical care to people regardless of their national affiliation, Daisaku Ikeda offers spiritual medicine to people so that the borders and barriers between human beings can be erased and an unprecedented era of human spirituality can occur.

Like Linus Pauling, Daisaku Ikeda has fought ferociously against nuclear weapons. As an absolute pacifist, Ikeda has vigorously campaigned the United Nations for the past thirty years for the abolition of nuclear weapons. Each year his treatise against nuclear weapons is read into the minutes at the United Nations.

Nobel prize winners such as Jane Addams (International President of the Women's International League for Peace and Freedom) and Baroness Bertha Sophie Felicita Von Suttner (President of Permanent International Peace Bureau) worked tirelessly for their vision of global peace. Ikeda has worked as indefatigably toward the same goal by elevating dialogue to a global level. Since the early 1970s, Daisaku Ikeda has convened dozens of dialogues of peace with artists, politicians, scholars, social activists, poets, sculptors, musicians, photographers, and museum directors from around the world. A short list includes: Henry Kissinger, André Malraux, John Kenneth Galbraith, Zhou Enali, John Major, Margaret Thatcher, Jiang Zemin, Kocheril Roman, Aleksei Kosygin, Fidel Castro, Lech Walesa, and Rosa Parks, and Nobel Prize winners such as Linus Pauling, Nelson Mandela, Mikhail Gorbachev, and Mikhail A. Sholokhov. Like Socrates in the agora (marketplace) of ancient Athens, Daisaku Ikeda searches for truth by dialoguing with the most intelligent and most influential people of his era.

In one way or another, every one of Dr. Ikeda's 125 books deals with peace, whether it is his children's stories or books featuring his world-class photography. Ikeda's diverse writings, which have been translated into over 20 languages, have reached a wide audience. His philosophical writings, essays, dialogues and addresses discuss art, peace, education, world hunger, spirituality, capital punishment, and numerous other topics. His poetry and novels have struck a spark in the literary world, so much so that the World Academy of Arts and Cultures named him its poet laureate in 1981. His children's books promote peace, love, and hope. Ikeda has successfully communicated his message of peace to an international, interfaith, and intergenerational audience.

2. The Burden of Introduction

A tremendous burden is put upon me: I am responsible for introducing the educational philosophy of Daisaku Ikeda to the Western world.

First and foremost, Buddhism pervades the thinking of Daisaku Ikeda. To understand why Ikeda advocates world peace, we must examine his Buddhist philosophy. Trying to understand Ikeda without understanding Buddhism is like trying to understand buildings without understanding architecture. For example, his idea of globalism is born from the Buddhist belief in the interconnectedness of all life.

Integrated into Ikeda's Buddhism are the educational theories of Tsunesaburo Makiguchi, first president of the Soka Gakkai (Society of Value Creators). Value-creating is fundamental to this philosophy of education; the more positive values brought into the world, the greater the meaning of life.

The full scope of the educational philosophy of Daisaku Ikeda is not expounded in any one definitive text. The task for the scholar is to reassemble Ikeda's insights into a streamlined whole. Ikeda's philosophy cannot be poured from the jar right into a pan. Nor is his philosophy fragmented, disparate ingredients to which other ingredients must be added. The basics of his educational philosophy are all there, but have to be seasoned slightly for their full flavor to emerge. My job as a scholar-cook is to season the wisdom just right to allow aromatic juices to blend.

3. Organization of the Book

To ensure fluidity, the text is divided into thirty-five short chapters. By design, chapters read like short essays. In theory, each one of these chapters can be detached from the text and can become the focus of a discussion or the theme of a class.

The book is divided into four major sections. In Part One, Ikeda's Buddhist beliefs are explored. Daisaku Ikeda is greatly influenced by the writings of Nichiren Daishonin, a 13th century Japanese priest who believed that all living beings have the potential to reach enlightenment. Another huge influence is Tsunesaburo Makiguchi, the first president of Soka Gakkai and one of the most controversial educational theorists in Japan in the early twentieth century. The first section of book also includes analyses of the five kinds of eyes, ten states of being, three thousand realms in a single moment of life (*ichinen sanzen*), three realms and ten factors, the causality of karma, the greater and lesser self, kōsen-rufu, value-creation, and enlightenment.

In Part Two, the major principles of Ikeda's philosophy of education are enumerated. They consist of inner revolution, cosmic citizenship, peaceful competition, completeness-incompleteness, philosophically based education, self-mastery, hope as a moral virtue, trust and harmony, faith and ultimate meaning, and the superrational.

The third part brings Ikeda into imaginary dialogues with some of the most influential thinkers on education, including Lao Tzu, Plato, Mill, Whitehead, Dewey, Gramsci, King, Freire, and Gardner. This will allow the reader to see how Ikeda's thinking on education intersects with some of the more influential ideas of philosophy of education. Part III and Part IV extend Ikeda's philosophy of education. "Meeting Today's Educational Challenges on Ikeda's Terms," the final section, discusses how Ikeda's philosophy of education—especially inner revolution—can counteract violence, low self-esteem, reductionism and compartmentalization, nihilism and apathy, and intolerance.

4. The Search for Wisdom: Spirituality in Education

How can Daisaku Ikeda's philosophy of education be of service to educators around the world?

One of the biggest perversions is the belief that spirituality has no place in education. Education prepares students for their careers and for becoming good citizens, while religion works on the spiritual aspect of the person. Education offers knowledge, religion wisdom. Teachers give technical not spiritual advice. This division is typical in a world full of divisions.

The search for wisdom is the search for spirituality. Spirituality is the act of searching for truth, beauty, goodness, and the ultimate source of what is. The objects of spirituality can be called wisdom.

Exiling spirituality from education means exiling wisdom. From the standpoint of today's spiritual aridity, that makes little sense. In education, spirituality is sometimes seen as the frosting on the cake. It makes the cake tastier, but isn't essential. Wisdom is treated as an accessory, much like a compact disc player in a car.

Functional education produces knowledgeable people. It does not cultivate wise people. Educational systems that produce students who merely function in an economic system create dysfunctional citizens. If we want people to become "better citizens," don't we mean that they should be tolerant and respectful of others, be willing to dialogue with others in order to work out differences, and be interested in the interconnectedness of states of affairs?

"Good citizenship" hinges on meeting each other as spiritual beings. For in our spirituality, our ideals and ultimately our greatness reside. The act of spirituality upgrades the human spirit, changing focus from the petty to the profound, from a self-serving limited scope to a community-focused far-sightedness. When we do not meet each other as spiritual beings, we meet as animals staking out our territories.

The largest religion in the world is Consumerism. Advertising spreads the gospel of Consumerism around the planet with remarkable speed. Commercials and commercialized programming are our children's teachers. Commercials, the new oracles of Delphi, deluge young minds with appeals to the baser instincts and foster materialistic dreams. Where is the true wisdom to counteract this "false" wisdom? Can a wisdom-based education be this counteracting force?

A wisdom-based education leads to the question that all generations must face: What is it to be human? How we answer that question determines our life philosophy, our morals, and the way we educate persons.

For the past fifty years Daisaku Ikeda has sought to answer that question. His work is more than the sum total of universities, high schools, grade school, cultural centers he has founded. His work is more than the sum total of the dozens of books that he has published. His work answers the question of

"What does it mean to be human?" with the answer: "To live peacefully with yourself, other people, and all beings in the universe."

5. Soka Education

In *Soka Education: A Buddhist Vision for Teachers, Students and Parents*, Ikeda identifies the fundamental questions guiding the core curriculum of Soka University of America in Aliso, Viejo California, the most recent university he has founded:

> What is the individual human life?
> What is the relationship between the individual and the physical environment in which we live?
> What is the relationship between the individual and human environment in which we live?
> What are the global issues in peace, culture and education?[1]

These guiding questions will be addressed from historical, multicultural, analytic, and experiential perspectives. More than offering a liberal arts education, Soka University of America distinguishes itself from many institutions in the following areas: creativity, value creation, happiness wisdom, egalitarianism, and Socratic dialogue.

"Creativity," Ikeda writes, "could be called the badge or proof of our humanity. Human beings are the only creatures capable of striving positively and dynamically, day after day, to create newer, higher, values."[2] Value-creating education helps people to produce benefits and remove harms, cultivate good and avoid evil, and to create beauty and repel the ugly.[3] The object of value-creating education is happiness. The world desperately needs an age of wisdom because information and knowledge don't necessarily produce happiness.[4]

An egalitarian and Socratic ethos should guide educational practices. As Ikeda says of faculty at Soka University of America: "They must respect and treasure the students as comrades and equals."[5] An egalitarian environment is well suited for open dialogue. Unless education is grounded in open dialogue, then "parochial perspectives and the passions" will reign.[6]

This humanistic, life-affirming educational philosophy implies much beyond its guiding principles. It implies concern for distant peoples and distant times. It implies a vision beyond global unity—it implies a cosmic unity. It implies new ways to assess wisdom, especially as it relates to the ten states of being.

More than explain the principles of Ikeda's educational philosophy, this book will discuss their implications. Ignoring their implications would mean harvesting a fecund intellectual crop without seeing what by-products could be extracted—certainly not in the spirit of value-creating education.

PART ONE

BLENDING BUDDHISM AND HUMANISM

One

THE BUDDHISM OF NICHIREN DAISHONIN

> If you wish to free yourself from the sufferings of birth and death you have endured since time without beginning and to attain without fail unsurpassed enlightenment in this lifetime, you must perceive the mystic truth that is originally inherent in all living beings.
>
> Nichiren Daishonin
> "On Attaining Buddahood in This Lifetime"
> *The Writings of Nichiren Daishonin*

1. Nichiren Daishonin and His Impact on Ikeda

The greatest impact on Daisaku Ikeda's thinking is from two sources: Tsunesaburo Makiguchi and Nichiren Daishonin. From Makiguchi, Ikeda learns the basics of a philosophy of education strongly rooted in twentieth-century humanism, which features value-creating. In the Buddhism of Nichiren Daishonin, this twentieth-century humanism and educational theory is nestled and nurtured. Josei Toda, second president of SGI, vividly and forcibly articulates the ideas Nicherin Daishonin and Tsunesburo Makiguchi to Daisaku Ikeda and becomes the vital link between those two thinkers and Ikeda.

Ikeda's philosophy is rooted in five aspects of Nichiren Daishonin's thinking: the possibility of widespread enlightenment, inclusion, social responsibility, dialogue as a method of discovering truth, and living a life of conviction.

Born to a poor fisherman's family in the village of Kominato, Nichiren Daishonin (1222-1282) revolutionizes Buddhism and pays the stiff price most revolutionaries pay: persecution. From 1253 until the end of his life, Nichiren Daishonin becomes a target of rival religious groups. Exiled and under the constant threat of death, he continues to proclaim that The Lotus Sutra is the only true doctrine of Buddhism.

The writings of Nichiren Daishonin consist of 172 works that have been translated into English, including his five major works. The revolutionary nature of his work (especially his assertion of the primacy of the Lotus Sutra) can be seen more clearly against the backdrop of the historical development of Buddhism and history of Japan.

My historical synopsis is drawn from Philip B. Yampolsky's Introduction to the *Selected Writings of Nichiren,*[1] Burton Watson's Introduction to *Letters of Nichiren,*[2] and the Foreword to *The Writings of Nichiren Daishonin.*[3]

2. The Buddhism Nichiren Daishonin Inherits

In the middle of the sixth century, Buddhism makes its first appearance in Japan as it filters down from Korea. The nature of this Buddhism is Mahayana, not Hinayana, at root.

For Hinayana Buddhism, the quest for each person is to realize personal salvation, nirvana, the state of supreme happiness. For Mahayana Buddhism, the quest is altruistic, focused on the liberation of all beings. The saint who achieves nirvana (*arhat*) is the ideal for Hinayana Buddhism. The wholly compassionate being, or bodhisattva, is the ideal for Mahayana Buddhism. The Mahayanist vows not to enter into final nirvana until all beings have been liberated. All aspects of Daisaku Ikeda's educational philosophy are pervaded and animated by this fundamental belief that our encounters with all beings be guided by compassion. His concept of globalism, for example, is guided by compassion instead of economic, political, and cultural hegemony.

As first practiced in Japan, Mahayana Buddhism consists of complex theories and monastic discipline and appealed to the aristocracy. The emergence of Tendai and True Word Buddhism in the eighth century, while insisting that all beings can reach Buddhahood, fails to bring this message to the people. Instead, their activities consist of elaborate myths, mystic rituals, and in-group and out-group disputes.

During the next four hundred years, a prevailing sense of pessimism, or nihilism, plagues Japan. The Mahayana doctrine stressing *mujo* (impermanence and ever-changing nature of life), meant to awaken people to seriously consider their salvation, mutates into the belief that change will inevitably bring change for the worse. This belief can be linked to the concept of the three ages of Buddhist teaching: the Age of Law (flourishing of Buddha's teaching), the Age of Decline (decay of Buddha's teaching), and the Latter Day of the Law (when the law loses the power of salvation). The political unrest and social decay of the time "proves" that thirteenth-century Japanese live in the Latter Day.

The dark cloud of Latter Day ideology discourages people from believing that they can achieve individual enlightenment in this life through their own efforts. In the time of degeneracy, only an outside power can enlighten people. This explains why at that time belief in the Buddha Amida becomes popular. Anyone reciting the simple formula of praise can be saved by the Buddha Amida, who whisks off his believers to a far-off land after death to enjoy eternal bliss. Two schools, the Pure Land School and the True Land School, arise around the belief in Buddha Amida.

Another form of Buddhism, Zen, also emerges. Zen becomes the religion of choice for shoguns of the twelfth century. Enlightenment could be reached by spending hours meditating in the lotus position. De-emphasizing learning and stressing discipline, Zen has a huge appeal to members of the military class. The Precepts School, a school of monastic discipline, also has a resurgence during this time.

Cut deep by the existential anguish of *mujo*, believing themselves to be living in the corrupt Latter Day, and fearful of social change, natural catastrophes, and foreign invasion, people cling to their religious beliefs. At this fragile time, the introduction of the radically new beliefs of Nichiren Daishonin can only be seen as a war against the lifeblood of civilization.

From the beginning of his study of Buddhism, Nichiren Daishonin (né Zennichi-maro) sees the potpourri of conflicting Buddhist beliefs and sets upon finding the ultimate truth. After studying the major Buddhist religions for over two decades, he concludes only The Lotus Sutra is the essence of Buddha's teachings—all other sutras are paths leading to The Lotus Sutra.

3. 1253: The Revolution Begins

The date is the twenty-eighth day of the fourth month of the year 1253. Here, Nichiren Daishonin chants *Nam-myoho-renge-kyo* three times. *Nam-myoho-renge-kyo*, the title of The Lotus Sutra (*Devotion to the Sutra of the Lotus Blossom of the Wonderful Law*), contains "the entire sutra consisting of all eight volumes, twenty-eight chapters and 69,384 characters without exception."[4] For Nichiren Daishonin, *Nam-myoho-renge-kyo* represents the ultimate truth and law consisting of all phenomena and the Buddha nature inherent in all life.

After his chanting, Nichiren Daishonin declares The Lotus Sutra to be supreme. *Nam-myoho-renge-kyo*, he asserts, is the only teaching that can lead people to enlightenment in the Latter Day of the Law. These pronouncements anger rival priests. Nichiren visits Buddhist temples to debate their chief priests. He criticizes Zen for rejecting the sutras and the Pure Land School for insisting salvation can be gained merely by invoking the name of Amida Buddha. Seven years later, in *On Establishing the Correct Teaching for the Peace of the Land*, Nichiren declares that worshipping false doctrines, specifically, the Buddha Amida, causes calamities in the country. Alarmed at his growing popularity, the Pure Landers attempt and narrowly miss assassinating Nichiren.

During a drought in 1271, when he learns that the respected priest Ryokan promises to produce rain through prayer, Nichiren sends him a challenge: if his prayers produce rain, Nichiren will become Ryokan's disciple; but if it doesn't, then Ryokan will become Nicherin's disciple. It doesn't rain, but Ryokan doesn't become Nichiren's disciple—instead a bitter enemy who conspires with other priests to bring Nichiren to trial. This leads to another attempted, but another failed, assassination attempt of Nichiren and ultimately to Nichiren's banishment to the island of Sabo.

In 1274, the priests of the Tendai temple arrange for a group of warriors to attack unarmed farmers, converts to Daishonin. When the farmers retain faith in the midst of torture and beheadings, Nichiren Daishonin becomes convinced that his people are now strong enough in faith to defend the Mystic Law. Thus, he inscribes *Nam-myho-renge-kyo* on a tablet, later called the Gohonzen.

4. The Egalitarian and Inclusive Nature of Enlightenment

In the philosophy of Nichiren Daishonin, all beings, animate and inanimate can achieve Buddhahood. "On Attaining Buddhahood in This Lifetime," he declares:

> If you wish to free yourself from the sufferings of birth and death you have endured since time without beginning and to attain without fail unsurpassed enlightenment in this lifetime, you must perceive the mystic truth that is originally inherent in all living beings. This truth is Myoho-renge-kyo. Chanting Myoho-renge-kyo will therefore enable you to grasp the mystic truth innate in all life.[5]

It doesn't take multiple lives to become enlightened, as it does with other Buddhist sects. Enlightenment is possible in this lifetime.

Ikeda aligns Nichiren Daishonin's concept of enlightenment with "human revolution." Enlightenment allows us to see and express our potential and flourish, the correct sense of Aristotle's *eudaimonia.* The enlightened life reveals truths about ourselves that allows us to live joyfully and meaningfully. This is consistent with the Mahayana Buddhist belief that enlightenment is innately in all beings.

According to Ikeda, human revolution, "changes arising the from the deepest strata of life," represent "the only way to a solution to mankind's dilemma."[6] Happiness is only possible through the inner search for truth, or self-revolution.[7] If external revolutions are to be successful, they "must arise from internal revolutions."[8] Ikeda states: "The time has come to take first priority away from exterior authority and give it to the revolution that must occur in the heart of each human being."[9]

In a famous passage, Nichiren Daishonin uses the analogy of a tarnished mirror to describe enlightenment of the soul. When the soul is tarnished by the illusions, it cannot reflect reality. When polished, it reflects reality:

> It is the same with a Buddha and an ordinary being. When deluded, one is called an ordinary being, but when enlightened one is called a Buddha. This is similar to a tarnished mirror that will shine like a jewel when polished. A mind now clouded by the illusions of the innate darkness of

> life is like a tarnished mirror, but when polished, it is sure to become like a clear mirror, reflecting the essential nature of phenomena and the true aspect of reality.[10]

Enlightenment begins by chanting *Nam-myoho-renge-kyo* to the Gohonzon and strengthening faith. Yet there can be no Buddhism without practice and study. The enlightened must teach others. This is the practice of Buddhism. The study of Buddhism is the third element of enlightenment. Practice and study arise from faith. Living an enlightened and altruistic life means leading other people to lasting happiness and building enduring peace for humanity.

In Nichiren Daishonin's Buddhism, all beings have the potential to be enlightened. This represents egalitarian and inclusive Buddhism. Enlightenment can occur in this lifetime. Enlightenment does not occur in faith, but through the triad of faith, practice, and study.[11] Following Nichiren Daishonin's Buddhism entails social responsibility, as we help others to become enlightened.

Daisaku Ikeda's philosophy of education reflects the basis of enlightenment as suggested by Nichiren Daishonin. All people on this planet, rich, poor, of Third or First World, male and female, are capable of enlightenment. Secondly, it is the responsibility of enlightened people to help others become enlightened. Translating this into educational pedagogy and social practice, this means that no being on this planet is incapable of being educated. All have the light within.

Another more subtle aspect of Nichiren Daishonin's Buddhism is dialogue. This is implied in the idea of the enlightened helping others to become enlightened. But as demonstrated in the life of Nichiren Daishonin, dialogue is the means for discovering truth. Nichiren Daishonin journeys to Buddhist temples to dialogue on his convictions. He simply does not accept them as truth. In some sense, this is similar to what Socrates did. Upon being called the wisest of all men by the Oracle of Delphi, Socrates questions the wisest people he could find in order to determine whether the oracle was right. This is also the mission of Nichiren Daishonin: "so long as persons of wisdom do not prove my teachings to be false, I will never yield! All other troubles are no more to me than dust before the wind."[12]

Living a life of conviction represents an important element of Nichiren Daishonin's Buddhism. Announcing truths to others and bearing the brunt of persecution that accompanies such announcements is an unstated part of this philosophy.

As we will see in the next chapter, the humanism of Tsunesaburo Makiguchi helps Ikeda to reinforce and extend Nichiren Daishonin's concept of enlightenment.

Two

The Humanism of Tsunesaburo Makiguchi

> On the basis of more than thirty years spent in the field of education, I would be hard pressed to think of any single group of people who are more concerned with their own self-preservation and less concerned with service to others than teachers. Only rarely will teachers set their sights beyond looking after number one long enough to consider the life of the nation or society at large. I can only feel disheartened and ashamed when I observe how few in the teaching community would even think to engage themselves in discussions of how to best the public interest, when not one misses the least opportunity to advance his or her own self-interest.
>
> Tsunesaburo Makiguchi
> *Education for Creative Living*

1. Challenging Authority

The life of Tsunesaburo Makiguchi (1871-1944) runs strangely parallel to the life of Nichiren Daishonin. Like Nichiren Daishonin, Makiguchi is born into a poor family and experiences poverty at other times in his life. Hopping from one job to another to support his wife and children, his life is also jolted by the deaths of four of his children during an eight-year period. His students call him *Fukuichi-chan* (one-suit man) because he wears the same kimono all year around. His egalitarian education theories reflect his concern for the poor. When he refuses to give preferential treatment to the rich, he loses his position as principal of Taisho Primary School.[1]

Like Nichiren Daishonin, he finds fault with fragmentation, in his case fragmentation within educational theory. Educational theory, imported from the West and grafted together like some kind of misshapen quilt, contributes to a meaningless educational experience for students whose primary activity is to memorize facts. Like Nichiren, he believes that enlightenment consists of self-awareness. Like his predecessor, he takes a stand against the status quo. He criticizes the Japanese educational system for failing to cultivate independent-thinking students and chastises teachers for being self-serving and focusing on the transmission of knowledge instead of the happiness of students. Like his predecessor, he is persecuted for his stand. Whereas Nichiren Daishonin is exiled, Makiguchi serves time in prison for his convictions.

As a young educator in the early part of the twentieth century, Makiguchi makes enemies by rejecting the prevailing view that the purpose of education (as defined by the traditionalists and Confucianists) is to create loyal and obedient subjects instead of independent thinkers.[2] His early work, *Jinsei Chirigaku* (*The Geography of Human Life*) examines the relationship of human behavior and geography. Like John Dewey, he favors the inductive over the deductive method. Whatever cannot be proved experientially can only lead to unending and unresolvable debates. In the same vein, teachers are to learn about teaching through their own teaching experience rather than applying general theories.

If 1253 is the turning point of Nichiren Daishonin's life, 1930 is the turning point of Makiguchi's life. He organizes the Soka Kyoiku Gakkai (Value-Creating Education Society), which becomes a formal organization in 1937. Makiguchi serves as its first president. In its first few years, the organization primarily consists of educators. By 1937, people from many different walks of life join the organization. The new membership can be attributed to a new religious aspect to the organization, as Makiguchi embraces the Buddhism of Nichiren Shoshu. In 1943, the Japanese government arrests Makiguchi, Josei Toda, and nineteen other members of Soka Kyoiku Gakkai for their opposition to the government supported State Shinto. In 1944 at the age of 73, Makiguchi dies in prison.[3]

2. *Humanist Manifesto I* and Makiguchi's Philosophy of Education

Makiguchi's philosophy of education stems from three sources: (1) geography (the relationship of learners to their geographic environments); (2) scientific method stemming from pragmatic orientation; and (3) sociology and anthropology."[4] Makiguchi's conversion to Nichiren Shoshu, while a dramatic moment in his life, does little to alter his pragmatic position, which he holds to the end.[5]

The overarching idea of Makiguchi's age is humanism. A broader examination of Makiguchi's philosophy of education entails placing it in the context of humanism, in particular, *Humanist Manifesto I*, a coherent synthesis of the ideas of that age.

Like most philosophies and religions, humanism can take many shapes and forms. At least eight forms of humanism can be identified: literary (devotion to the humanities); Renaissance (rediscovery of classical works and renewed confidence of human beings to discover truth on their own); cultural (rational and empirical tradition of ancient Greece and Rome); philosophical (outlook of life focused on human need or interest); Christian (barebones of Christianity buttressed by Renaissance humanism); modern, naturalistic, scientific, ethical, or democratic humanism (naturalistic philosophy rejecting all supernaturalism); secular (outgrowth of eighteenth-century enlightenment and nineteenth-century free thought); and religious (outgrowth of Ethical Culture, Unitarianism, and Universalism).[6]

Some of the dominant characteristics of humanism include:

(1) In embracing a naturalistic metaphysics based on reason and scientific method, it rejects the supernatural.
(2) Death ends life.
(3) Human beings can solve their own problems.
(4) Rejecting determinism, it makes human beings masters of their destinies.
(5) The good life consists of self-development contributing to the greater good of society.
(6) Humanism promotes democracy, peace, and economic prosperity for all nations and peoples.
(7) As a philosophy of compassion, humanism is concerned with meeting human needs and human problems and considers among its virtues, tolerance and fellowship.
(8) Humanism elevates the cultivation of art and awareness of beauty to the forefront of human experience.
(9) Far from dismissing intuitive feelings, inspiration, emotion, altered states of consciousness, and religious experiences, humanism wishes to to reduce them to rationality.
(10) Morals come from human beings, not a divine source.[7]

Perhaps the most succinct and inclusive definition of humanism is rendered by the American Humanist Association: humanism "is a rational philosophy informed by science, inspired by art, and motivated by compassion."[8]

In the Introduction to Makiguchi's *Education for Creative Living*, Dayle Bethel identifies six aspects of Makiguchi's philosophy of education: purpose in education, happiness, value creation, student responsibility, science of education, and the integration of school, home, and community in the learning process.[9] Yet Makiguchi's educational theory is attuned with the greater intellectual movement of humanism in 1933, *Humanist Manifesto I* was signed by many of the leading intellectual of the era, including John Dewey. As the opening paragraph of the *Manifesto* states:

> The time has come for widespread recognition of the radical changes in religious beliefs throughout the modern world. The time is past for mere revision of traditional attitudes. Science and economic change have disrupted the old beliefs. Religions the world over are under the necessity of coming to terms with new conditions created by a vastly increased knowledge and experience. In every field of human activity, the vital movement is now in the direction of a candid and explicit humanism.[10]

A. Specific Needs, Specific Philosophies of Life

According to *Manifesto I*, human beings are products of their particular cultures; they develop because of their interaction with the natural environment and social heritage: "The individual born into a particular culture is largely molded by that culture."[11] Makiguchi believes that the purpose of education theory must arise from the particular: "It [the purpose of education] must take into account the entire scope of human life, but at the same time must consider the specific needs of family, society, and nation."[12] Philosophies of life arise from the needs and demands of a particular society in the past and may "have been appropriate for that society at that time."[13] Yet a philosophy of life from another age may not be relevant for our age.

Purpose in education arises from context.

B. Happiness as Individual Fulfillment and Shared Experience

Manifesto I affirms that the end goal in life is human satisfaction: To foster "the complete realization of human personality to be the end of man's life" and cultivate the creative in man and to encourage achievements that add to the satisfactions of life."[14] Furthermore, "The goal of humanism is a free and universal society in which people voluntarily and intelligently cooperate for the common good." Against a profit-driven society, *Manifesto I* asserts:

> The humanists are firmly convinced that existing acquisitive and profit-motivated society has shown itself to be inadequate and that a radical change in methods, controls, and motives must be instituted. A socialized and cooperative economic order must be established to the end that the equitable distribution of the means of life be possible.[15]

Humanists demand a shared life in a shared world. Likewise, Makiguchi asserts that happiness consists not in a narrow, selfish pursuit for material possessions, but in the creation of value that elevates individuals and society: "Society is not a mere aggregation of people but their mental and spiritual union."[16] Education is not focused on material self-satisfaction, but "on spiritually uplifting the community."[17] Makiguchi is not looking to extinguish individualism, but to extend it to the full human framework. Whereas in the United States, *idividulualism* (satisfying materialistic needs) wins out over the development of the whole person, for Makiguchi happiness is equated with people creating a full spectrum of value in their lives.[18]

Via their spiritual bond or interaction, individuals are to society as cells are to a living organism. A society will only be as strong as its individuals:

> Where there is individual growth and fulfillment, there will be prosperity, enrichment, and health within the society as a whole. On the other hand,

> when the individual is stifled, the society weakens and deteriorates. A society prospers when its elements, or individuals, are united in their value commitments and disintegrates when wide divergence develops in those commitments.[19]

The complete realization of human personality, its self-realization, is attained through happiness. What Makiguchi means by happiness is similar to what Nichiren Daishonin calls enlightenment. Happiness and enlightenment occur when fully positive human potentials are actualized.

C. Value Creation

Human beings are creative. The cultivation of the creative in *Manifesto I* coincides with what Makiguchi calls value creation. While human beings cannot create matter, they can create value. Joy in our lives is directly related to creation of value in our personal lives and those whose lives we intersect.

Makiguchi firmly believes that education should become a science. Seeing the fragmentary and eclectic Japanese system borrowing contradictory theories from Western systems, Makiguchi wants to utilize objectivity (empirical data) to discover the correct methods. The primary goal of educators is to develop activities and curricula that will foster active involvement of persons in the creation of value. Understanding the laws of value creation, by studying exemplars of value-creating, is "an educational aim deserving our utmost attention and earnest efforts." [20]

Value creating is basis for happiness.

D. The Reorientation of Responsibility

Makiguchi calls for teachers to be role models. They are not mere transmitters of knowledge, but enlighteners in the purest sense of that word. As enlighteners, teacher hold a prominent position. They are the wise women and men who have a moral obligation to stand for ideals. Teachers must not be hypocrites; their words and actions must match. This is why Makiguchi maintains that "the notion of a profession called teaching presupposes that the teacher stand as an exemplary human being, a guidepost on the road of life."[21] Yet their importance is not a "holier-than-thou" importance. The fundamental aim

> of education is not to transfer knowledge; it is to guide the learning process, to put the responsibility for study into the students' own hands. It not the piecemeal merchandizing of information; it is the provision of keys that will allow people to unlock the vault of knowledge on their own.[22]

Humanist Manifesto I drops the responsibility of learning into the laps of individuals: "Man will learn to face the crises of life in terms of his knowledge of their naturalness and probability."[23] As Makiguchi says, people should unlock their own vaults of knowledge. The *Manifesto* goes a little farther than Makiguchi does in eliminating worship and prayer, but he suggests that when issues are ambiguous we must make our decisions rather than running to the shelter of our elders' untested perspectives. But in the same spirit of *Manifesto I*, of encouraging people to face the brave new world, Makiguchi envisions education as the cultivation of evaluation and appreciation to benefit student lives:

> When education realizes its important responsibility to conduct students in the creation of benefit values, it will look at the natural and human realms with different eyes in its search for subjects to teach. Mere cognitive intellectual interest will no longer be a sufficient criterion; the view to cultivating powers of benefit-value creation will come to the fore, bringing the curriculum around to include evaluative and appreciative courses on means of benefiting oneself.[24]

3. Makiguchi's Philosophy of Education: A Brief Evaluation

Makiguchi tackles one of the sensitive questions that many educators ignore: Is the purpose of education to create independent thinkers or to foster loyalty and obedience to the state? How this question is answered goes a long way in determining how teachers and students interact in the classroom.

If the purpose of schooling is for the production of loyal and obedient subjects, then loyalty and obedience must be fostered. The first way in which that is fostered is by students being obedient to teachers. Obedience often stifles critical thinking. Teachers set up a curriculum that is assumed to be sacred. Teachers are interpreters of the sacred texts. Obedience means that teachers control the flow of information and the activities of students. The essence of obedience is to what or to whom are we obedient.

The issue of loyalty is thornier than the issue of obedience in philosophy of education. Loyalty can be caricatured as "blind loyalty," as images of soldiers, political conventions, and religious ceremonies come to mind. Loyalty can also be seen in a positive light, as deep-seated commitment to a person or a cause. Yet in the classroom, when loyalty obliterates the search for truth, then a grave issue arises.

If the purpose of schooling is to produce independent thinkers, then the classroom takes on another air. This is not to say there isn't obedience in such schooling. Instead of being obedient to causes, countries, or teachers, students are obedient to the search for truth. There can be no sacred texts that only priestly teachers can interpret. Teachers become partners in the classroom, co-inquirers.

Teachers cannot temper students' search for truth by interposing any loyalty clauses. This does not mean, from Makiguchi's perspective, the classroom is without prime directives except for the search for truth. The quest for individual happiness is never solitary, but is based on interdependencies.

In most areas of human experience, people of the same profession do a poor job evaluating each other. For fear of retarding professional advancement, rocking the boat, or out of loyalty for the profession, people of the same profession often treat each other with kid gloves. One of the most refreshing aspects of Makiguchi's thought is his overt criticism of teachers. As the quotation at the outset of this chapter suggests, teachers often fail to look much beyond their classroom in their preparation of students. The larger world is not often in their plans.

This will be taken as an insult by many educators, a depreciation of them and their profession. While Makiguchi criticizes teachers of his era, he does not criticize teaching. Teaching for him is a noble profession. This point cannot be overemphasized. The popular quote of George Bernard Shaw, "He who can does. He who can't, teaches," declares that failures in life wind up in teaching because they can't do what they really want to do. Therefore, education is a second-rate profession. Makiguchi, however, recognizes the importance of teaching, its vital role to developing fulfilled human beings and cultivating wide-scale happiness. His ire is directed toward educational institutions and teachers who don't recognize their larger and more important role. Human potential is lost when educators ignore their larger purpose.

Ironically, the larger and more important role of teachers deprives them of their priestly roles as interpreters of the ancient texts. The larger and more important role of teachers is to create conditions under which students can flourish in their enlightenment. Teachers are to use their own best experience in the schooling to determine classroom practices.

Education that merely equips students to fit into a specific economic system ignores the total flourishing of the human person. Economic flourishing is but one aspect of human flourishing. From Makiguchi's perspective, human wealth consists of the creation of values, not the creation of capital.

The life of Tsunesaburo Makiguchi bears witness not only to educational theories, but also his ethical comportment. He remained an outspoken critic of the educational system and the Japanese government. He believed strongly in the value of fairness and was willing to lose his job to uphold that value. He strongly believed in independent thinking in an era when such proclamations earned him a jail term. Knowing all these things about the man, we can easily see why Makiguchi suggests that "respectable character" is the primary quality of teachers, who have such a great impact on children:

In the case of educators, however, entrusted as they are with the weighty responsibility of schooling tomorrow's citizenry and passing on today's culture to those who must assume leadership, it is important not only to prevent harm from coming to others' children but also that they actively work to show each child his or her potential to realize an ideal life.[25]

Three

FIVE KINDS OF EYES

> The power of science is intrinsically natural. It is nonetheless important to decide whether human beings ought to regard science as absolute or limited. This decision becomes an essential basis for independent thinking. . . .
>
> Man may no longer draw irresponsible optimistic conclusions about the future on the basis of science and technology alone. In fact, solutions cannot be sought in technical and material revolutions outside man but must be found in a reformation of humanity from within.
>
> Daisaku Ikeda
> as quoted in N. Radhakrishnan,
> *Daisaku Ikeda, The Man and His Mission*

The thinking of Nichiren Daishonin and Tsunesaburo Makiguchi is a response to the fragmentation in their respective eras. The twentieth century is also an era of fragmentation. Two world wars and the brutal Holocaust atrocities ruptured the twentieth century. This represents the ethical fissure of the twentieth century. Transportation and technology breakthroughs make us reevaluate the phrase "the four corners of the globe." Being able to gallop from one side of the globe to the other in a matter of a few hours, and to be able to instantaneously communicate with each other, makes the term "global village" a virtual reality. This represents the cultural fissure of the twentieth century, a challenge to tradition. The fragmentation of culture is complemented by technological fragmentation. New technology compels people to constantly readjust to the world. There is no one place where people can settle. A person's personal history and a civilization's collective history is no longer a set of discrete events, but a blur. When the substance of the past is a blur, tradition finds it hard to take root. Technology has changed the way we eat, play, learn, and commune with one another. A third fissure is the intellectual fissure. No philosophy sums up the intellectual fissure better than postmodernism, which celebrates irrationality, ambiguity, fragmentation, the anti-theoretical, and discontinuity.

Pluralistic reality is upon us—acceptance of the validity of diverse ideas and cultures. Yet this pluralism is moving by us so rapidly (like the characters on a slot machine) that we can barely discern it. If *ad nauseam* pluralism exists, then what is the educational response? What is the educational response for a generation looking for wholeness? These questions represent a good introduction to five eyes, or the five ways Buddhists say we look at the world.

The five different kinds of eyes are: the eye of humans, the eye of heaven, the eye of wisdom, the eye of the Buddhist Law (*dharma*), and the eye of Buddha.[1]

The eye of humans is focused on physical observations. This is ordinary sense perception. The eye is focused outwardly, to the world.

On the other hand, the eye of heaven turns inwardly to discern the delicate changes of the human mind. Instead of physical observation, the eye is turned back to mind. This is reflection.

The eye of wisdom or the eye of science synthesizes the first two eyes. It sees more than an array of objects, as the eye of humans does. Through the power of abstraction, it discovers universal laws

From the Western perspective, there are only three eyes. Usually, the breakdown is: Sense Perception, Understanding, and Reason. Reason (equivalent to the eye of wisdom) tends to be the most acute eye. But according to Buddhism, the eye of the Law is even more discerning. It can penetrate the truth of life more profoundly and from a more humanistic approach, and can see all things as they are.

Finally, the eye of Buddha penetrates the truth of life at its most profound level, uniting wisdom and compassion. Discerning the pulsating energy of life and all aspects of the universe, the beholders of the eye of Buddha become part of the universal life force and use this reactivated vital force to perceive realities of life, society, and universe and their interconnectedness. This is what is realized in the chanting of Nam-myoho-renge-kyo.

In spite of intellectual fragmentation, the prevailing view sees the highest form of knowledge as a kind of detachment from the world. When we abstract from something, we literally "draw away" (*abstrahere*). This "drawing away" is a distancing from the center of life:

> When scientific method works, as it always does, from analysis to generalization, some peculiarities and individual traits of the phenomena being observed are lost. For example, things that cannot be treated in quantitative terms or that cannot be universalized are discarded. When the object of study is humanity, the individual workings of the mind and spirit and the subtle characteristics of emotion and consciousness are rejected.[2]

For Buddhism, the summit of wisdom is not attained by pulling ourselves out of the world into a realm of abstraction. Penetrating the secrets of life means becoming part of life and not placing ourselves outside of it. The fundamental difference between the eye of the Law and the eye of Buddha emboldens the distinction between observing and participating. The eye of the Law shows us things as they are and in a more humane way than the eye of wisdom. The eye of the Law is more discerning because it is more connected to the universe. The eye of Buddha is even more discerning than in the eye of

Reason because its compassion is not from the outside looking in, but is an intimate compassion.

The eye of the Buddha is more than intellectual acumen. It is a blending of the heart and mind. Looking at the universe abstractly, we remain aloof from its workings. It remains mysterious to us because we fail to connect with it.

In a world of fragmentation, the eye of science subdivides the world into more compartments. The eye of science creates more fragmentation. The eye of Buddha brings us back into the world. It brings us face-to-face with truth. Being face-to-face with truth is not simply knowing truth, but being truth. Nichiren Daishonin encourages us to polish our mirrors day and night so that we may reflect reality. Yet we cannot reflect reality unless we become reality. In becoming reality, we overcome fragmentation and are able to approach a holistic perspective.

Facing a fragmented world, students need something sharper than the eye of science to grasp the whole. They require a pedagogical approach that brings them in communion with the world. The detached eye of science is a hardship to actual communion and holistic experience. Compassion is requisite for such a communion. Compassion brings us back to the larger world and beyond the singular hopes of billions of individuals to the collective hopes of humanity.

Reason becomes even sharper when blended with compassion. As Ikeda maintains:

> Only by first cultivating and activating the eye of the Law and the eye of the Buddha is it possible to transcend the essential limitations of scientific thinking as a function of the eye of wisdom and to cause science to emit an even more brilliant light of reason.[3]

Four

THE TEN STATES OF BEING

> Buddahood is, in short, the condition of absolute and indestructible happiness.
>
> Daisaku Ikeda
> *Unlocking the Mysteries of Birth and Death: Buddhism in the Contemporary World*

1. From the Prison of Hell to the Eternity of Buddahood

The experience of human beings has largely been oversimplified. Existentialists reduce our existence to anguish. The famous id-ego-superego of Freud is another reduction, as is Plato's reduction to reason-spirit-appetites. Beings-toward-death, naked apes, and featherless bipeds are other examples of reduction. Reductions of human nature to religion, economics, or aesthetics are also prevalent. In contrast to reductionism, the Buddhist conception of the ten states of being demonstrates the richness of human experience. The human experience is a combination of the ten states such that one may dominate over the others at a particular moment. The interpenetration and fluidity of the ten states renders an accurate description of the vicissitudes of the human emotional life. The ten states of being demonstrate the evolution of human spirituality from its lowest to highest levels. The first three states (hell, hungry spirits, animals, and *asura* or warlike demons) are called the four evils. The ten states are not watertight compartments, but portals through which human experience constantly flows.

Ikeda's *Life: An Enigma, a Precious Jewel*[1] and *Unlocking the Mysteries of Birth and Death: Buddhism in the Contemporary World*[2] are the basis of the following descriptions of the ten states of being. These insights have been drawn from *Great Concentration and Insight*, the masterpiece of T'ien-t'ai, a sixth century Buddhist thinker from China.

A. Hell (The First Evil Path)

Hell is the nadir of human experience. The blind rage of hell lashes out at everything and hits nothing. The profound agony of hell is the feeling of helplessness, as everything seems to be beyond our control. Unable to move or act freely, we experience a debilitating anger that we are utterly helpless to do away with evils of the world such as war, pollution, incurable illness, poverty, and family strife. Rage is not directed outward but at the self. This is the greatest kind of spiritual starvation. In hell, time stands still and each moment feels like an eternity.

B. Hungry Spirits (The Second Evil Path)

The spiritually starved are greedy and want to devour everything. This hunger is clearly seen in the drives for money, power, pleasure, and fame and the emotions such as greed, miserliness, and jealousy. Whereas in the state of hell, we feel helpless and believe everything is out of our control, in the state of hunger, we often control the world with the least spiritual of our faculties (greed, miserliness, and jealousy) and seek least valuable of goods (money, power, pleasure, fame). Hunger can work for good as well as for evil. For example, the hunger for industrialization has ended famine in most civilized nations. Yet hunger is characterized by an incessant yearning for what is just beyond our reach. In art, the greedy are portrayed with distended bellies and needle-thin throats. The road from the four evil paths does not always take an upward swing toward Buddhahood. For example, after eating poisoned meal, we might find ourselves back in hell. We might skip to anger if our desires and impulses are in conflict.

C. Animals (The Third Evil Path)

In the world of Animals, survival instincts dominate. This is translated into the law of the jungle. Whoever is weaker we dominate; whoever is stronger we flatter. In this state, the biological need of satiety may be fulfilled, but spiritual joy is lacking. While instincts help us to adapt to our environments, they fail to help us adapt to changing situations and cannot help us when confronted by higher intelligence. This is why the instincts unguided by reason are foolish.

D. *Asura* or Warlike Demons (The Fourth Evil Path)

Angry people have a perverse desire to subordinate others and see everything as a threat to their survival. Unlike the instinctive state, the anger state involves awareness of self. We value only ourselves; everyone else is demeaned, held in contempt. The sense of superiority is a defense mechanism against inner doubts and failing self-esteem. Anger is directed toward others to destroy them in order to preserve the self. In the state of anger, exhibitions of benevolence, righteousness, propriety, wisdom, and faith are just that—exhibitions. They mask the contempt just beneath the surface. Angry people appear to be bigger than life: their anger extends their being. They appear to be belligerent, warlike demons. In truth, the extended life-space is an illusion, a device used by angry people to wreak havoc.

E. Human Beings

The state of humanity, where people respond passively to their environments, is tranquil. We can live in a complete state of peace and happiness. The steady and peaceful flow of time accompanies this world. Humanity is characterized by intelligence, excellence, acute consciousness, sound judgment, superior wisdom, the ability to distinguish truth from falsehood, attain enlightenment, and a good karma from the past. The realm of humanity is towards the middle of the ten states because one can easily fall back into the four evils or ascend to the higher states.

F. Heavenly Beings

In the state of heavenly beings, exhilaration makes us feel so light that we believe we can soar into the sky. Enraptured, we often feel an abnormal sense of our own well-being, power, or importance. Enraptured, we are happy to be alive, and believe that everything is right in the world and nothing can harm us. Called the realm of the gods, this state consists of the joy of expanding our freedom, self-realization, and creativity. There is intense satisfaction of the desire to rule, to be honored, to possess things. Buoyed by a vigorous life force, enraptured people perceive their life-flow flying past them. While in the state of Human Beings, subjective time and measured time (minutes, days, months, years, etc.) are perceived as the same, in this state, subjective time is perceived to move much more rapidly than measured time. Rapture compresses time. A single day in the state of rapture may be equivalent to a hundred years in the state of humanity. While rapture is intense, it is short-lived and influenced by external factors. While desire does not pervade rapture as it does the first five states, it still touches the sixth state. The desires of the earlier states are fulfilled in rapture. Rapture is at the borderline between the world of form and the world of formlessness, between the material and spiritual worlds. The Devils of the Sixth Heaven, personifications of the evil, sit at the peak of desire. They manipulate Heavenly Beings by controlling and even destroying of the lives of others. The Devils of the Sixth Heaven can turn the benefits of technology into detriments. For example, technology can help feed the people of the world or to subdue them with weapons.

G. Voice-Hearers

In the six lower states or Six Paths, people's lives are dictated by the external environment. They flip-flop among the six paths as they are completely as the mercy of external factors. In the six lower states, we fail to realize that our lives are based on transient factors. In the state of Voice-Hearers (the first of the four Noble States), we recognize the impermanence of all phenomena as we reflect on the paths our lives have followed. The eye turns from the outer world to the inner life. The state of learning consists in learning through others in order to enlighten the self about the transitory nature of all things and futility of being absorbed in the impermanence. We absorb learning and wisdom from our predecessors, but so that we can boast how much we know instead of enriching the spirit.

H. Cause-Awakened Ones

Cause-awakened Ones discern the operation of the causal law in all phenomena. This realm is considered to be one of the partial realization or understanding. Cause-Awakened Ones gain understanding through observation of their environments. Their insights might be scientifically significant (theoretical insight into the workings of universe); poetical (metaphorical insight into the flowers blooming in a field or bright stars in sky); moral (value insight into the evil odor of a polluted river); or pedestrian (insights on how make ends meet, the right thing to say, or being able to handle a project). Without a long and deep study of life as a whole, such epiphanies would not be possible. For Cause-Awakened Ones and Voice-Hearers, happiness ascends to the highest level because it is not based on external factors, but on our own efforts to realize it. In both states, life-space is much greater than in the first six states, expanding to such a degree that we can have worlds of our own. Yet both states can still fall prey to evil, though they are filled with wisdom, happiness, and enlightenment. This is because people have not transcended selfishness, and the pride and loss of humility often attached to it. Using their brilliant insights for selfish reasons, they can cause much more harm than can people from the lower realms.

I. The Bodhisattva Nature

Compassion and altruistic nature comprise the Bodhisattva nature. Bodhisattvas not only want to achieve supreme enlightenment, but they want all other people to achieve supreme enlightenment as well. Compassionately connected with others, Bodhisattvas see solitary happiness as illusionary and seek to alleviate suffering in other people's lives. The strength of compassion is an energy flowing from inner depths of human life. Completely altruistic, it fuses together intelligence, love, determination, and valor. For Bodhisattvas, alleviating the suffering of others and bringing them happiness is a means of self-realization, a means to improve their character and find happiness. Bodhisattvas must have courage to challenge sources of evil; without courage they cannot overcome diabolical elements within themselves and others except by defeating evil forces. Bodhisattvas act to change the world. In the Bodhisattva state, we manifest the Buddha within us.

J. Buddhahood

Buddahood is the perfection of the Bodhisattva state. The ten titles of Buddhahood are actually ten character traits. Knowing the law causality running through the past, present, and future, the Buddha is thought of as coming from the world of truth. ("Thus Comes One"). Qualified to receive offerings from human and heavenly beings makes the Buddha "Worthy of Offerings." Knowing all phenomena correctly is described as "Right and Universal" and for understanding the past, present, and future and executing deeds to perfection is deemed "Perfect Clarity and Conduct." For communing in the world of enlightenment and the title "Goodness Attained" is applied. "Understanding the World" is designated for understanding all secular and religious affairs. Standing supreme among all other human beings is described as "Unexcelled Worthy." While "Leader of the People" refers to leading all people to enlightenment, "Teacher of Gods and Humans" refers to guiding all human and heavenly beings to enlightenment and "Buddha, the World-honored One" pertains to a person with perfect wisdom and virtue.

In the state of Buddahood, every activity directed toward benefit of others. The energy of compassion gushes forth from innermost source of life. Buddhas are well-integrated persons with a strong sense of responsibility and strong faith. They are friendly toward others and able to think flexibly, rich in compassion. Their life-force increases limitlessly. Joy, the indescribable ecstasy, wells up freely and spontaneously from the innermost essence of life. The life-space of Buddhas become united and fused with the universe; life-flow reaches out to encompass all that is past and future. In the lives of Buddhas, each moment is an eternity. They are hardly conscious of passage of time because life is full and happy at each instant. Buddhas understand all things of the universe impartially and regard them with equal compassion.

Five

THREE THOUSAND REALMS IN A SINGLE MOMENT OF LIFE

Perhaps nowhere do we find a better exposition of this idea, that the individual and the Cosmos are inseparable, than in the principle of *ichinen sanzen*, which has it that a single moment of life possesses three thousand realms.

Daisaku Ikeda
Unlocking the Mysteries of Birth and Death: Buddhism in the Contemporary World

1. The 3,000 Possible Worlds or *Ichinen Sanzen*

In each of the ten states of being, the other ten are latent. Thus, the ten worlds actually consist of 100 worlds. Each of these 100 worlds exhibits the ten factors: appearance, nature, entity, power, influence, internal cause, external cause, latent effect, and their consistency from beginning to end. These 1,000 worlds appear within the three realms of existence: the realm of the five components that constitute a living being, the realm of a living beings, and the realm of the environment.[1]

2. The Three Realms

Form (body and sensory organs), perception (function of sense organs to receive external information, conception (forming ideas about sense data), volition (will to act in response to the received and conceived), and consciousness (exercising value judgments) constitute the five components, one of the three realms. Except for form, the rest are considered spiritual aspects.[2]

Whereas the five components pertain to the physical and psychic analysis of living beings, the realm of living worlds pertains to the continuous interrelationship and reciprocal influence among livings beings. The realm of living beings not only pertains to the physical environment but to the social environment as well.

The realm of environment pertains to the environment that supports the existence of beings. This consists of the mostly non-sentient environment: example, oceans, mountains, and plants.

3. The Ten Factors

The Ten Worlds represent expressions of life, the emotional life. The ten factors represent the ontological categories of life.[3]

The first three of the ten factors view life from a static perspective. Appearance refers to the external aspects of phenomena, their physical aspect: the color of a person's eyes, their height and weight, and the way they act. Nature refers to the spiritual aspects of phenomena. This means what cannot be discerned through an internal inspection. What we would normally call the mind and consciousness of another person. Entity is neither appearance nor nature, but manifests itself in both. It is changeless reality, like a soul.

The other seven factors are dynamic aspects of life. Power is potential strength or energy to accomplish something, for example, in the state of Bodhisattva, we have the potential to alleviate the sufferings of other people. The action or movement of power in thought, speech, or action is called influence.

The cause latent in life that simultaneously contains a latent effect is called the internal cause. Internal causes can create effects of the same nature as themselves. Power and cause can be distinguished in the following way. Power arises without any external mediation, whereas internal cause must be stimulated by an external cause. The auxiliary cause is called the external cause or relation. External cause relates life to its surroundings. The internal cause and latent effect occur simultaneously. On the contrary, the manifest effect is the perceivable result that is the consequence of the internal cause and latent effect. The internal cause of an acorn is its potential to grow into an oak tree. External causes (sun, rain, soil) contribute to the simultaneity of internal cause and latent effect. Having the potential to be means possessing the cause and effect. The manifest effect is the observable result of the internal cause and latent effect. This observable result appears over the course of time.

The tenth factor is consistency from beginning to end. Consistency is the integrating factor uniting the other moments of life. Where there is one factor, all other nine must be present.

4. The 3,000 Worlds and the Holistic Person

The Buddhist conception of *ichinen sanzen* offers a complex yet vivid depiction of human nature unlike any western conception.

It's a platitude to say that human reality is complex, but the theoretical response to this platitude has often been models of human nature that reduce human experience and human nature to one or a few realms. Nor do these models do an especially good job at demonstrating the interrelationship and dynamism of human reality.

Ichinen sanzen is a perhaps the most accurate depiction of the complexity of human nature and human reality in the history of philosophy. The basic human emotional attitudes (Ten Worlds) are integrated with our cognitive faculties, interactive and reciprocal relationship with other beings, support of the non-sentient environment (taken collectively, the Three Realms) and intersect ontological realities (the Ten Factors). The uniqueness of human existence is dramatically portrayed in the *ichinen sanzen*. To fully understand what it means to be human, the driving question of wisdom-based education, we require a model based on the *ichinen sanzen* that helps us determine our place in the chain of being.

Six

THE CAUSALITY OF KARMA

We can no longer regard karmic disease and its cure as matters just for the individual. Mankind as a whole has accumulated a horrific amount of evil karma, symbolized by our obscene stockpile of nuclear weapons, use of a small fraction of which would spell the end of all land-based life on the planet.

Daisaku Ikeda
Unlocking the Mysteries of Birth and Death: Buddhism in the Contemporary World

Karma (action) means that all of our physical, verbal, and mental actions eventually affect us at some future date.[1] Initially, the effects remain latent. Yet eventually they will fully emerge whether in this life or others. Our evolution toward the higher states of being depends upon an acute understanding of karma.

If I murder another person, I produce a chain of causality whereby I will someday be harmed. If I save another person's life, then I produce causal nexus whereby something good will occur. If I am verbally abusive to another person, then eventually those words will turn back on me. If I affirm another person, then at some future day my words will benefit. If I am insanely jealous of another person, then those thoughts will harm me. If my mind is filled with compassion for others, then they will have a positive effect on me. Everything we do, say, or think has an effect on us. While this effect may remain latent for an extended period of time, eventually it emerges.

Karma can be categorized in the following ways. When actions arise from good intentions, kindness, and compassion, this is good karma. Evil karma, on the other hand, arises from actions induced by greed, anger, and stupidity. While present karma refers to karma we have made and whose effects will appear in the present life, past karma refers to karma formed in previous existences. Immutable karma is karma that produces a fixed result; mutable karma is karma whose result is not absolutely fixed and whose effect is not set to appear at a predetermined time.[2]

As a theory of causality, karma is more sophisticated than simple cause and effect schemes. Cause and effect isn't limited to physical actions, but extends to verbal and cognitive actions. Cause and effect is not limited to a single lifespan but spills over into future lives. We accumulate karma from life to life. The old saying "You can't take it with you" doesn't apply to karma.

Karma follows us from one life to the next. Karma is causality that transcends the barriers of time and space.

Karma places full responsibility on individuals. Other people or the environment cannot be blamed for our failings. We are responsible for anything that happens to us. When bad things happen to us and we scratch our heads wondering what we could have done to deserve it, the event can be understood as bad karma inherited from a past life. Karma is not the doing of a transcendent being. Thus, God cannot be blamed for our predicaments.

Karma challenges our freedom. Human beings have freedom to the extent we can alter our karma. Such freedom demonstrates good karma in previous lives. The very fact that we have been born as human beings indicates that we have the potential to alter the course of our lives, no matter how tainted by evil karma, so that they are filled with good karma. Being able to change our karma constitutes our dignity as human beings.

If individuals fail to transform bad karma into good karma, then societal and global attempts to realize justice will be futile:

> Our lives are marred by the deadly influence of poisonous man-made substances, from food additives to industrial wastes. Another problem is the degradation of the human spirit, resulting in upward-spiraling violence and the ever-increasing search to gratify egoistic desires. All of these negative aspects of our lives—and we could list many others—can in the broad sense be considered symptoms of humanity's collective accumulation of evil karma.[3]

Poverty, AIDS, and war cannot be wiped away with a single act. The gargantuan breadth and baroque complexity of these evils continue to accumulate. On a global and historical scale, mankind has created bad karma for thousands of years. Wars, oppression, and genocide represent one aspect of this karma. This is called shared or general karma. Another aspect is the vile and hurtful words that people have said to one another. Another aspect is the jealous, vengeful, and malicious thoughts that people have had about one another.

Viewed in this way, the bad karma on the global and historical level is immense. As Ikeda states, the latent effects nuclear weapons, pollution, and greed will eventually bear fruit.

Everything we do bears fruit, according to the karmic perspective of the world. Everything we do, say, or think matters. We are also responsible for the fruit we bear. Whether the fruit is sweet or sour depends upon our actions at the moment. Consequently, all our acts are meaningful and everything matters.

Seven

THE NINE CONSCIOUSNESSES AND THE GREATER AND LESSER SELF

> The greater self of Mahayana Buddhism is another way of expressing the openness and expansiveness of character that embraces the sufferings of all people as one's own.
>
> Daisaku Ikeda
> *A New Humanism*

Mahayana Buddhism distinguishes between two selves: the greater and lesser self. The lesser self is concerned with the petty, transient things of life, while the greater self reaches out into and connects with the cosmos. Buddhist philosophy focuses on transcending the lesser self and expanding consciousness toward the greater self.

The first five consciousnesses represent the five senses: seeing, hearing, smelling, tasting, and touching. The sixth consciousness integrates and categorizes sense perception. While the sixth consciousness relates to physical objects, the seventh consciousness or mano-consciousness (*manas* = mind, intellect, or thought) operates independently of outer experience. Mano-consciousness distinguishes between truth and falsehood and good and evil and is capable of reflection and abstraction. In mano-consciousness, self is discovered. But the discovery of self is often accompanied by illusions of the self, including its absolute and unchanging nature, self-attachment, and conceit. Mano-consciousness, though rational like the sixth consciousness, is primarily a deep, unconscious awareness of self. Mano-consciousness gives birth to sexual, aggressive, and instinctual drives, the cause of delusions, but also good faith, feelings of repentance, and intellectual faculties such as wisdom and perseverance.[1]

The eighth layer of consciousness, *alaya*-consciousness, is a dwelling or receptacle for all the thoughts, words, and actions of the first seven consciousness. These imprints are the seeds for the future; they are karma, the potential our actions to produce effects in the future. Accumulated in our *alaya*-consciousness are experiences from previous lifetimes. The eighth consciousness is equivalent to the Bodhisattva state in which karma formed by compassion and altruism battle evil karma. After death, the tendencies in our lives as illustrated by the Ten Worlds become frozen. Those of us who tend to spend most of our lives in hell or hunger will merge with the hell or hunger realm of the cosmic life realm.

But more than an individual's own karma, *alaya*-consciousness contains karma common to one's family, race, or humanity as a whole, containing memories of our human and pre-human ancestors. This may be thought of as a kind of collective unconscious, of which all phenomena, not just human beings, share.

The *alaya*-consciousness includes purity and impurity. It represents a region where good and evil do battle. Even the alaya-consciousness is fraught with illusion. A ninth consciousness, a pure, stainless, spotless, or *amala*-consciousness, is posited as the ultimate and unconditioned reality. This is the universal Buddha nature in which we become one with the life-flow of the universe. Thus, the *amala*-consciousness represents the greater self. In worshipping the Gohonzen and chanting *Nam-myoho-renge-kyo*, we experience the ninth consciousness and kinship with the universe.

The *amala*-consciousness is that sees itself as part of the cosmic flow of the universe. This is the self that infinitely expands, in contrast to the narrow self of the first six of the Ten Worlds and the first six consciousnesses. In *mano*-consciousness, subjective space increases as we turn away from immediate reactions to the world of the senses:

> Lasting happiness as taught by Buddhism is derived from giving oneself to immutable truth perceived beyond ceaselessly changing phenomena. The process whereby this happiness is achieved can be thought of as the search for the truth within the self, or self-revolution.[2]

When we reach the greater self of *amala*-consciousness, we see beyond the particulars of the sense world and have a more profound grasp of reality. Only when we are greater selves can we see that:

> The question of the kind of life human beings ought to lead cannot be solved within the framework of accepted social commonplaces and mere common sense. This is true because man himself is not limited to a single society in a single country but is part of a chain connecting humanity, the natural phenomena of the whole earth, and the cosmos.[3]

The greater self is the universal self, a self breaking down all barriers: between person and person, nation and nation, animate and inanimate being. Not fused to the universal flow of life, the lesser self is imprisoned in the world of the senses, which show it boundaries and limitations. United with cosmic flow, the greater self is knows no boundaries. It experiences deep kinship with all beings.

The lesser self is consciously attuned issues of life related to the four evil paths, while the greater self attuned to higher levels of being The more spiritual we become, the more we ascend toward *amala*-consciousness and Buddahood, the more cosmically connected we become.

Eight

KŌSEN-RUFU

What is our goal?
Is it *kōsen-rufu*
In pursuing it we must surmount countless obstacles
This dedication and the long campaign to spread the teachings
shall be our lifelong journey.

Daisaku Ikeda
"Song of Youth," in *Songs from My Heart*

Translating *kōsen-rufu* as happiness or peace reduces it to a state when *kōsen-rufu* is more accurately thought of as an action. *Kōsen-rufu* is "the means of securing lasting global peace by propagating true Buddhism and bringing people to enjoy indestructible happiness."[1] To widely declare and spread Buddhism is its literal meaning.[2] Ikeda adds another layer of meaning to *kōsen-rufu*: revolution. This revolution is inner revolution, beginning in each person.

In "Song of My Youth," Ikeda identifies three kinds of revolution: political, economic, and educational. The failure of these revolutions is because they are not revolutions of human spirit and are thus "one-sided":

In the past there have been different kinds of revolution
political, economic, educational
But when one type of revolution is carried out in isolation
it lacks solidity, gives rise to strain and onesidedness
A political revolution alone
calls forth bloodshed, insures no safety for the populace
and once again those in authority lord it over the masses

Likewise economic revolution
fails to fulfill the hopes of the people
the penniless commoners are trampled underfoot in a process of
meaningless change
A revolution in education only
again is not blessing to the people—
it cannot bear up before the turmoil of the world's shifts and movements

What the people long for
to carry them through the twenty-first century
is not reorganization of external forms alone[3]

External changes in political, economic, and educational systems are the wrong places to begin successful and sustainable revolution capable of bringing about *kōsen-rufu*:

They desire a sound revolution
carried out within themselves
gradually and in an atmosphere of peace
founded upon the philosophy and beliefs of each individual
This calls for farsighted judgments
and a profound system of principles

This is what I would name a total revolution
and it is this
we call *kōsen-rufu*[4]

Kōsen-rufu arises but does not culminate in individual persons. It culminates in igniting revolutionary enlightenment in others. As Buddha says:

> "Though I attain Buddhahood, I shall never be complete until my affirming light reaches all over the world. . . .
>
> "Though I attain Buddhahood, I shall never be complete until people everywhere determine to attain Enlightenment, practise virtues, and wish to be born in my land." [5]

Inner revolution is the ascent through the ten states toward Buddhahood, which can only be accomplished as we tap into the fundamental reality of the world. Through the chanting of the *Nam-myoho-renge-kyo*, we tap into the fundamental reality of life and recognize, on both a compassionate and intellectual level, the interconnectedness of everything. The enlightenment of Buddha is the integration of the intellect and heart.

Kōsen-rufu begins in the enlightenment of each person, but culminates in the enlightenment of all beings. External revolutions, political, economic, and educational revolutions, build weak foundations that can only temporarily support human flourishing. Internal revolutions can provide a solid and lasting foundation for human flourishing. Enlightenment based on the compassionate recognition of the interconnectedness of all things is the cornerstone of a society in which human flourishing is not limited to one time (ancient Athens), one class (nobles or First World countries), or extraordinary individuals (Leonardo da Vinci). Ikeda's vision of *kōsen-rufu* includes: "The support of complete knowledge/ the foundation of complete democracy/the soil of complete culture."[6]

Kōsen-rufu is the supreme good of human existence. It reflects the Mahayana belief that the enlightened are compassionate persons who help others achieve the same degree of enlightenment. Not a static state, but a dynamic flow, *kōsen-rufu* is vital universal happiness of peaceful co-existence.

Kōsen-rufu can function as the ultimate goal for a world in which apathy and cynicism fester in the human soul and render human beings "immune to the emotions of love or hatred, suffering or joy."[7] As many philosophers have said, the human spirit seeks completion and k*ōsen-rufu* represents the fulfillment of moral completion.

Nine

VALUE CREATION

> Human values must never be narrow: they must never be oriented toward satisfying only the aims of individuals, groups, races, nations, or ideologies. Human values must be universal. In the past narrow values have led to tragedy. In the life of each individual lurks karma and greed. In the lives of all persons engaged in creating any society are unfathomable destinies, all of which overlap and interweave to form reality.
>
> Daisaku Ikeda
> as quoted in N. Radhakrishnan,
> *Daisaku Ikeda, The Man and His Mission*

Run-of-the-mill humanism advocates compassion and care about the overall happiness of humanity. Where such humanism fails is that it lacks an ontological and epistemological basis for motivation. Buddhism provides that basis. The ontological affirmation of the spiritual connectedness of all beings and the epistemological affirmation that in the highest state of knowledge we can grasp this connectedness provide a viable ethical foundation. Philosophies of deconstruction, empiricism, and language analysis are poor vehicles for the justification of the ethical message of humanism. For these philosophies hack reason to pieces, barely affirming consciousness exists.

Makiguchi believes we attain happiness by creating value: "A happy life signifies nothing but the state of existence one can gain and create value in full."[1] He identifies three kinds of value: beauty (what brings aesthetic fulfillment to a person); benefit (what advances a person's life in a holistic way); and goodness (what contributes to well-being of the larger community).[2]

Buddhism provides Ikeda with a means of expanding Machiguchi's perspectives about the relationship between individual and community. Narrow values are egocentric values. They never escape from the long shadows of our selfish desires exemplified in the worlds of hell, hungry spirits, animals, and warlike demons. The closer we come to Buddhahood, the more universal our values. The compassionate wisdom of Buddhahood grasps the interconnections of all things not from the perspective of a distant, detached scientific eye, but from the perspective of a Good Samaritan:

> Controlling egoism and delusion for the sake of all living beings, they consider creating value for the lives of others and for the global

> biosphere their own reason for living and indeed the supreme way of life. For this reason, their actions are always altruistically inspired.[3]

A "universal" order failing to generate such ethical values as humility and generosity must be recognized as false and deceptive. The absence of such values indicate a failure to reach Buddhahood. In Buddhahood, humility, generosity, and values such as trust create positive values. Only by tapping into the ultimate reality deep in our souls can we reach our full potential as human beings.

Ten

ENLIGHTENMENT

> Partial enlightenment leads to pride and loss of humility. To the partially enlightened one, only his vision is correct.
>
> Daisaku Ikeda
> *Life: An Enigma, a Precious Jewel*

From the humanist perspective, enlightenment stems from the evolution of reason: our greater understanding of the universe, scientific achievements, and deeper appreciation of brotherhood, as is stated in *Humanist Manifesto I*. This trinity faintly resembles the compassionate wisdom of Buddhahood. The humanist conception of enlightenment has attributes of the states of Human Beings, Heavenly Beings, and Voice-Hearers. To characterize such enlightenment as equivalent to the keen compassion Bodhisattva state would be negligent. In the enlightenment of Buddhahood, wisdom and compassion are interwoven. In humanist enlightenment, the evolution of reason does not include the emergence of compassionate wisdom. In western tradition, reason is often segregated from emotion. Humanism sees through the eye of science, but not through the eye of Buddha (the deeper integration of wisdom and compassion).

From the Mahayana Buddhist perspective, enlightenment can but may not necessarily be realized in one lifetime. Enlightenment might take several lifetimes to achieve. Karma accumulated from other lifetimes affects us in our present existence, but the karma we accumulated in this lifetime can affect us in this existence or future existences. In Mahayana Buddhism, causality extends beyond this and into others. The idea of karma is a mystical notion that is incompatible with humanism in principle. *Humanist Manifesto I* discourages unreal hopes and wishful thinking about the supernatural. The Buddhist view of karma fits under this category.

For Mahayana Buddhism, enlightenment can, but may not necessarily, be realized in one lifetime. Humanism is dismissive of mystical unions of this nature and sees it as an atavism of traditional and outdated religions. From the standpoint of humanism, Buddhist enlightenment is misguided. From the standpoint of Buddhism, humanism is shallow, incomplete, and unevolved. The compassionate wisdom of Buddahood is predicated on the most profound understanding of the universe: communion with the underlying reality.

In contemporary education, the humanist conception of wisdom is prevalently taught. This diluted form of wisdom is characterized by separating reason from compassion, reason from mysticism, and reason from spirituality. Enlightenment as described by Nichiren Daishonin and Daisaku Ikeda encompasses all faculties of human cognition and represents richer possibilities of educating people.

The new humanism of Daisaku Ikeda—spiritual or cosmic humanism—introduces a new wrinkle to humanism that reflects the current converging state of science and religion. When *Manifesto I* was written, science and religion were going their separate ways. The Scopes Trial exemplifies this parting of the ways. But as the new millennium has dawned, scientists are starting to speak like theologians, theologians like scientists. Science and religions may not have become bedfellows, but they are beginning to intertwine. If such intertwining is to be reflected in the philosophy of humanism, it is to re-examine and re-evaluate the supernatural element, long since discarded on the waste heap of antiquated ideas.

PART TWO

IKEDA'S MAJOR PRINCIPLES AND VIRTUES

Eleven

COMPASSIONATE REVOLUTION

> [H]uman beings are the true starting-point and that, to be long-lasting, all external revolutions must arise from internal revolutions.
>
> Daisaku Ikeda
> *Choose Peace: A Dialogue between Johan Galtung and Daisaku Ikeda*

In the overall and educational philosophy of Daisaku Ikeda, internal or spiritual revolution is the overarching concept: "The process whereby this happiness is achieved can be thought of as the search for the truth within the self, or self-revolution."[1] The five basic precepts of revolution are: (1) the beginning of all revolution is the spiritual revolutions of individuals; (2) spiritual revolutions lead to a larger conception of self reflecting the interconnectedness of all things; (3) revolutions altering physical, social, or technological conditions can only be partially successful; (4) the ultimate aim of revolutions is a civilization based on Bodhisattva principles of compassion; and (5) while revolution begins with the enlightenment of individuals, it culminates in the enlightenment of all people and all beings.

The first step in revolution is not changing external, but internal, architecture:

> Man cannot hope to find happiness in revolutions, in systems and technology alone. For many years I have been insisting on the vital importance of what I call a human revolution because I am convinced that changes arising the from the deepest strata of life are the only way to a solution to mankind's dilemma.[2]

Spiritual architecture is often built on shaky foundations, in particular, the four lower worlds (hell, hungry spirits, animals, warlike demons). These tumultuous states render the architecture of the outer world unstable. Unless spiritual architecture has a solid and lasting foundation, social and political architecture never will.

Successful revolutions are based on a thorough understanding of human nature. Without understanding the struggles within, revolutionary change can only occur in fragmented and piece-meal way:

> All past revolutions have devoted insufficient study to the basics of human nature and have attempted to rebuild society by means of reconstruction of no more than systems and institutions. It is true these revolutions have succeeded in some fields, but it is their very lack of

> attention to human nature that has caused them to fail in bringing about a total renovation of man's society.[3]

The ultimate goal of inner revolution is to create a civilization around the principles of a Bodhisattva way of life:

> Revolutionizing the individual and society along the lines of the Bodhisattva way of life promised hope for the future. People of Bodhisattva frame of mind are aware of the whole world and therefore feel deep concern for everything in the biosphere—even beings concealed by distances in time or space. Such Bodhisattvas could unite to form a solidarity of citizens of the Earth. And a mass movement of wise, compassionate people who keep posterity always in mind could build a society that respects human dignity and rights, and prizes creativity in its scientific, economic and legal systems. The birth of such a society would signal, the dawn of birth of a century of life.[4]

Revolutionary education would include an attitude of total affirmation of the Bodhisattva state:

> In all epochs, in both East and West, outstanding teachers have always adopted an attitude like that of "Never Despising" in dealing with students. Just such an attitude ought to be the foundation of education systems, structures, and concepts. Ensuring it such a place will demand an extraordinary revolution. But, if achieved, the revolution can change the way of thinking and living of individuals and of all society.[5]

Inner revolution is an ascent toward our innate Buddha nature. Spiritual revolution is an ascent through the four evil paths and toward the Bodhisattva state and Buddhahood. The eye of Buddha is not simply highly developed reason, but the integration of reason and compassion. The ascent from the lower states to the higher states implies recognition of the interrelatedness of the self with the universe. People "must comprehend the relation between his own life and the life the universe because only making this revolutionary discovery can he find the true path of real joy and real compassion that can shed its warming grace over the whole world."[6]

All human beings have the potential for inner revolution. The influence of Nicherin Daishonin and Tsunesaburo Makiguchi is deeply evident here. Human beings can enlighten themselves. Teachers help ignite enlightenment, but are never the source of that enlightenment. Education must give human beings back to themselves. Contrary to models of learning that encourage students bow before external authorities, Ikeda's model of education turns people inward to internal authority: "The time has come to take first priority away from exterior authority and give it to the revolution that must occur in the heart of each human being."[7]

While revolution begins with the individual, it does not end with the individual. The truly revolutionary human being helps others achieve enlightenment. This is not because of a sterile moral imperative to help others. Full enlightenment consists of fully—intellectually and spiritually—recognizing our bond with all beings in the universe. We identify the self with the universe. Consequently, the higher levels of wisdom expand self from our physical needs to the needs of other beings, whether sentient or nonsentient.

Ikeda's conception of revolution is an extraordinary beginning to a philosophy of education. Its implication to curriculum and classroom practices is staggering. A shift in curriculum must take place: from information-based to wisdom-based. The primary objective of education is for students to ascend toward an expanded understanding of self. Classroom practices, including the teacher-student relationship, should reflect wisdom-based education. If students continually look for teachers to validate them through the usual incentives (grades, scholarships, the prospect of high-paying jobs), then a wisdom-based education cannot be realized. The task of a teacher is to help students turn inward so that they can judge their own progress. In human revolution, individuals are responsible for assessing their own spiritual growth.

Twelve

COSMIC CITIZENSHIP

This will be the society no one has ever seen before
The homeland that everyone has sought

Then men for the first time
will emerge from the shiftings of the dark night
to return to themselves
and mankind too
will reach the oasis, reversion to the primal

Daisaku Ikeda
"In the River of Revolution"
in *Songs from My Heart*

The best way to describe the kind of citizenship that Ikeda proposes is to use the term "cosmic or cosmopolitan citizenship." Terms such as "globalism" and "global citizen" are insufficient to catch the Ikeda's meaning. "Globalism" and "global citizen" have negative connotations, especially from those who see globalism as economic globalism and see it as veil for the expansion of American capitalism or of a world government authoritatively imposed on people, "fascism with a smile." When Ikeda refers to "cosmic humanism" in *A New Humanism*, he alludes to an enlightened citizen in the Buddhist sense, with an expanded notion of self.[1]

The path to cosmic citizenship begins "by delving vertically into the inner layers of one's own mind" and coming "upon universality."[2] Expanding upon the idea of Argentine poet Jorge Luis Borges, Ikeda describes the vertical plunge into our minds as inner revolution and enlightenment. The horizontal plane is the external political world. Where the vertical and horizontal worlds meet represents is the juncture where the cosmopolitan citizen emerges. While retaining autonomy, the cosmopolitan citizen possesses a universal outlook. Understanding and consensus are the means for attaining cosmic citizenship.

Ikeda envisions an interconnecting of humanity that at the same preserves local customs: "The only way to create global unity is to build a world civilization linking together all humanity which, while preserving and making positive use of local traditions, at the same time, is truly international culture."[3] Only the cumulative wisdom of all peoples can solve global problems: "A unified global system for the twenty-first century requires the aggregate wisdom of all peoples."[4]

Ikeda's vision of ideal society excludes special interest groups or sects. In his startling poem "In the River of Revolution," Ikeda declares:

We have no need of any sect
Valorously transcending the obstacles
of narrow partisanship, of cliques,
as human beings
as stark-naked human beings,
live, move, and for the sake of the joyous new society
fight, young man!
And I too will fight![5]

The only sect worth preserving is the human sect:

The sect of nonsectarianism
the sect called human-being, which is no sect at all-
let us call this the Human Party[6]

Cosmic citizenship depends upon "vertical" enlightenment and recognition of true self, the true image of ourselves as interconnected with all beings:

But when you stand
upon that silent, artless, and fathomable Dharma,
the solemn essence
that flows beneath the *Sein* of
the universe, the world, and human life,
then for the first time that clouded mirror hidden within you
will shine, be wiped clean,
and reflect the true image of you yourselves[7]

"Globalism" and "global citizenship" often fall on the deaf ears of students reared on narcissistic consumerism. The "Me First" attitude of consumerism is incompatible with the "shared world" perspective of cosmic citizenship. The cosmic citizen is not first and foremost hungering and hankering for the acquisition of new things and political power to gain even more new things. The endless appetite of consumerism and its continuing pursuit of external goods makes it a poor foundation on which to base cosmic citizenship. Tribal self-interest can only be transcended with a deeper understanding of what the nature of the self is, what reality is. This requires the eye of Buddha, the ultimate synthesis of wisdom and compassion.

From Ikeda's perspective, cosmic citizenship demands cosmopolitan education. Sprinkling diversity into the curriculum is not the way to foster feelings of connectedness. The ultimate feeling of connectedness occurs in the vertical recesses of our minds and grasping the greater self.

Thirteen

PEACEFUL COMPETITION

> The focus of the thinking will determine everything that follows. Men are capable of conceiving ideas that are grand and lofty, and those that are petty and mean. Therefore, there is not need to despair just because the realities of the situation seem forbidding. Man is never entirely without hope; in this respect he is a very fortunate animal. Where there is thinking that is correctly oriented, there will be correct ideals, and correct ideals will surely lead to correct government.
>
> Daisaku Ikeda
> *Glass Children and Other Essays*

In the philosophy of Buddhism, thinking correctly oriented toward peace reflects enlightenment and the Buddha nature. Peace among people is a reflection of peace within individuals. Self-aggrandizement, governments limiting citizen participation, and exploitation are not the wrong routes to peace:

> Is the point to be simply the advancement of oneself as an individual, or is it to the cause of world peace? Is it to be the maintenance of power of one particular class in society, or, even worse, the venting of hatred and the invasion of another country?[1]

The route to peace is the actualization of the greater self. Business activities lacking the greater self will not contribute to peace: "If business activities are to contribute to efforts toward peace, the logic of capital must be tempered by the logic of humanity."[2] Yet competition, correctly conceived, promotes peace: "Since competition, in its constructive sense, spurs progress, I believe that the best way to attain world unity and peace is for nations to compete in what are really character-building activities."[3] This stands in stark contrast to competition manifested in the war economies:

> It will be necessary to break up the traditional war economy and move to an economic structure that can preserve peace. In this way, the vast sums now spent on nuclear development and armament expansion can be diverted to the uses of peace and prosperity.[4]

In principle, peace is the ultimate state of freedom. Stability is secured, while individual creativity flourishes. Ikeda wants to devise a system that provides stability, peace, and universal justice without interfering with the freedom and creative potential of the individual. In a climate of peace, pure individuality flourishes.

One of the more peculiar aspects of Ikeda's thinking is the relationship between competition and peace, which he borrowed from Makiguchi. For this correlation to work, we must see competition in its best sense, as an activity between persons or groups designed to bring about improvement on both sides. In this sense, competition is a "win-win" scenario. In some sense, competition contains elements of cooperation: its Latin root is *competere*, "to strive together." The contemporary sense of the word emphasizes the idea of winners and losers and deficit and gain. The ideology of capitalistic competition depicting economics as war is often based on principle of "Get him before he gets me" philosophy. In such an environment, war is a way of life, not optional.

"Striving together" toward peace is a "striving together" in the Mahayana sense of helping others to attain enlightenment. "Striving together" is a moral imperative of the Bodhisattva state and an ascendance toward Buddahood.

Peace is not a state of inertia, but an empathetic-sympathetic striving-together. It is state of vital human connectivity representing the crown of human spiritual accomplishment. Peace can be conceived a state of complete affirmation, in which practice the "Never Disparaging" Bodhisattva philosophy.

One of the greatest challenges in peace education is to encourage responsibility for building peace in the future. Peace is a multi-generational process. Short-sighted persons with little feeling for future generations can hardly be expected to make much effort to bring about peace in their age. "That's their problem" is the view of short-sighted people. Self is limited to a physical body at specific spatio-temporal coordinates.

A greater sense of self is imperative for peace studies. Without seeing ourselves as integral parts of a long chain of human beings striving toward peace, we lose our desire for peace. The hope for piece is connected to the belief of being part of the process of contributing to peace. The hope for peace is really the predominant hope for the future. From the Buddhist perspective. whatever causality we bring into the world in this life we have to deal with in the next.

Daisaku Ikeda reiterates that global peace will emerge slowly and after many struggles. For that peace to emerge, long-term policies will have to be adopted. The commitment to long-term policies runs counter to the commitment to short-term pleasures and quarterly earnings. Without becoming far-sighted, human beings cannot expect to find the right routes to peace. Perhaps the largest challenge in "teaching peace" is cultivating a sense of connectedness not simply with "diverse" people, but with the future. Whereas the Oedipal conflict is a centerpiece of psychoanalysis, the future conflict is the centerpiece of peace studies. Correctly oriented ideals do not perish with the death of the physical body, but exist as the supreme hopes for all human beings. Even in epochs where peace seems impossible, the ideal of peace must be over-nighted to successive generations.

Fourteen

COMPLETENESS AND INCOMPLETENESS

> The reifying nature of language destroys the dynamic synergy of completeness and incompleteness.
>
> Daisaku Ikeda
> *A New Humanism*

For Daisaku Ikeda, the creative life of Leonardo da Vinci is a metaphor for explaining the synergy between the completeness of incompleteness and the incompleteness of completeness of the dynamic nature of reality. While Leonardo began many projects in his life, he completed few of them. One of ways to look at these partly finished works is to say that while observers believed them incomplete from the Leonardo's perspective they were finished. Ikeda suggests "the completeness of incompleteness is simultaneously the incompleteness of completeness."[1]

This apparent paradox reminds us of the famous dictum of Heraclitus, that the way and the way down are the same. For Heraclitus, opposites can only exist if they exist together. Concavity only exists because convexity exists, and vice versa.

Ikeda takes the completeness-incompleteness paradox in another direction. In attempting to make the invisible world visible or the universal particular, something is lost. As a concrete thing, the work of art will always be a particular, incomplete. In the same way, there are no perfect circles in the world, there are no perfect works of art. Works of art remain incomplete.

Creativity is that movement toward the next creation, toward completion. Incompleteness is just as much a part of completeness as completeness is part of incompleteness. For Ikeda, incompleteness and completeness give rise to life activity: "From the completeness of incompleteness to the incompleteness of completeness—the synergy between these two perspectives is the source of life's infinite creativity, the dynamism of existence."[2]

The synergy of completeness-incompleteness is evident in thinking. Thinking is simultaneously a movement toward order and toward chaos, toward clarity and ambiguity. Clarity points toward completeness; ambiguity points toward incompleteness:

> Thinking is not simply the movement from ambiguity to clarity, but from clarity to ambiguity. In other words, it is a double movement. Clarification is one element of thinking, but equally important is the movement back to ambiguity, toward chaos. Thinking is a tension between pulling together and pushing apart.[3]

The work of art and the nature of thinking dramatize the dynamic movement of all things. Existence is fluidity, not solid. Yet language often obscures fluidity from view: "The reifying nature of language destroys the dynamic synergy of completeness and incompleteness and creates the illusion that a temporary state of stability is eternal."[4]

Lao Tzu warns:

> Therefore the intelligent man accepts what is as what is. In seeking to grasp what is, he does not devote himself to the making of distinctions which are then mistaken to be separate existences.
>
> In teaching, he teaches, not by describing and pointing out differences, but by example.[5]

A danger of naming is the illusion of the stability language. This occurs as names become categories and categories become closed systems. Categories are often seen as fixed truths.

The mania for naming and classifying distracts us from the primary activity of wisdom: discovering of the fundamental truth of completeness-incompleteness. As Lao Tzu suggests, those who are more concerned with grammar miss the meaning of words:

> If we stop fussing about grammatical trivialities, we will get along much better.
>
> The difference between "Yes" and "Ya" is insignificant compared with a genuine distinction like "Good" and "Bad."
>
> Yet some people are as fearful of making a grammatical mistake as of committing a vital error.[6]

In the same way dangling participles can be ranked as more important than catastrophic rises in global population, so the activity of naming can be ranked as more important than discovery of primal reality.

Primal reality is not a fixed or complete system and like poetry

> /is/more/than/the/sum
> of/its/parts[7]

Yet schooling often fails to convey the dynamic and paradoxical implications of the number one obvious fact of reality. This is a primary reason why wisdom is stunningly absent from schooling:

> Socrates, where are you? Will you come forward? Buddha, where are you? Will you speak up? Gandhi, where are you? Will you come in?

Why do they stand there?
Why don't they come in?

Because everything is still and static
Everything stays the same.

Wisdom stays
In the halls
Until learning
Learns all its flaws.[8]

Fifteen

SELF-MASTERY

> Our society today urgently needs the kind of inwardly directed spirituality to strengthen self-control and restraint.
>
> Daisaku Ikeda
> *A New Humanism*

Religions and moralities are often like stop signs and stoplights at intersections: without them, accidents would happen. Cars would crash into each other; disputes would be common; causalities would occur. Stop signs and stoplights are external standards that tell us when to stop and when to go.

Acting in accordance with external standards means conforming to them and often failing to reflect on their true nature and whether they are right or wrong. Discipline of the self is necessary to abide by external standards, but discipline of the self is different from self-discipline. Discipline of the self is pragmatic and externally directed. We discipline ourselves to follow rules that other people have set up for us. Self-discipline is self-imposed. We discipline ourselves to follow rules we set up for ourselves.

The evil in human nature can be controlled: "Because human life includes both good and evil, it is necessary to stimulate the unlimited growth of the good sides of human nature and to attempt to control the bad sides."[1] The greatest spiritual achievements arise from control of desires: "Learning to control them [desires] wisely and to preserve nobility in our humanity is the starting point of such elements of spiritual culture as ethics, morality, philosophy, and religion."[2] The great treasures of spirit cannot be discovered except through compassionate interaction lending itself to the exchange of ideas.

External benchmarks such as technological and scientific advances have been the norm. The only way for people to gain true independence is self-control. The paradox of trying to control the outer environment is that without self-mastery it can turn back on us and enslave us:

> For many years I have been insisting that progress deals solely with the external material world. It is now time for us to turn our eyes to humanity's inner aspects. We must reaffirm our own independence by controlling and guiding the artificial environment we have created instead of allowing ourselves to be controlled by it. In order to have the kind of wisdom needed

> to accomplish this, the human spirit must be filled with the pulsing force of universal life that permeates humanity, nature, and all things.[3]

Ikeda is optimistic that inner revolution and enlightenment can bring about the transformation of discipline of self to self-discipline. He sees this as an inherent attribute of Mahayana Buddhism:

> Northern Buddhism ultimately seeks social reform through individual enlightenment. It holds that, by translating the Buddhist spirit of compassion into action for this ultimate cause, the individual can not only control but also transform his desire into constructive spiritual forces.[4]

Rationality is not the pinnacle of self-control: "Reason is clearly incapable of controlling all the phenomena of the force of life. Love, hate, happiness, anger, sorrow, and joy are all beyond its control."[5] Ikeda believes the highest form of spirituality, the eye of Buddha, is the core of inner strength:

> Morality is generally thought of as the way to control one's innate evil. However, it tends to be an intellectual matter, and human evils involve emotion more often than reason. I believe that religion, which delves deeper into human life than the rational mind, must be the source of the inner strength to control evil and facilitate life on a high moral and ethical plane.[6]

The highest form of spirituality and enlightenment is compassionate awareness of the underlying unity that binds all of life together.

The more spiritually enlightened we become, the more compassionate. In the Bodhisattva state, self-control is altruistic:

> Controlling egoism and delusion for the sake of all living beings, they consider creating value for the lives of others and for the global biosphere their own reason for living and indeed the supreme way of life. For this reason, their actions are always altruistically inspired.[7]

A visible of self-control in social relationships is the rise of culture and the decline of force. The logic of power is externally imposed, while the power of culture is based on creativity:

> The fundamental nature of culture is accord and harmony. It is diametrically opposed to force, especially the force of arms. While military power threatens humanity and imposes control from without, culture arises from within the human mind as a liberating force. Furthermore, the logic of power

> assumes the militarily and economically strong nations will conquer smaller and weaker ones. By contrast, cultural exchange requires the positive acceptance of another's viewpoint, the autonomy of the recipient is a necessary condition. Finally, military power is geared toward destruction, whereas culture is premised on creativity.[8]

Ikeda wants no stoplights and stop signs at intersections. Each enlightened person knows when to slow down, yield, and stop. Personal responsibility begins with personal enlightenment. Schooling trying to cultivate personal responsibility and enlightenment cannot place stoplights and stop signs at every corner. Classroom micromanaging, holding a carrot in front of students in the form of grades, praise, or future materialistic success, fails to cultivate self-mastery required to ascend from the lower states toward the higher states of being.

Sixteen

PHILOSOPHICALLY BASED EDUCATION

> It is my hope and my conviction that we will see a revival of philosophy in the broadest, Socratic meaning of the word.
>
> Daisaku Ikeda
> *A New Humanism*

The search for wisdom is not conducted in isolation, but in dialogue. Dialogue is a vehicle for self-illumination and revolution of the self. Dialogue is a litmus test for our ideas. Even the deepest convictions must be tested by dialogue. An idea not seriously tested by dialogue is an idea destined to become illusion. From Ikeda's perspective, the most effective schooling is based on dialogue in the Socratic sense. Socratic dialogue leads to deeper examination of the self and ultimate questions of reality—the nature of the universe. For Ikeda, "This truth is deeper still than the truths of general philosophy: it is the ultimate of the universe and of all life itself and is the meaning of Nam-myoho-renge-kyo."[1]

Without a wisdom-based approach geared to exploring the vertical levels of the self, education fails. For Ikeda, "the absence of a leading philosophy renders human beings incapable of discovering deep values and makes them the rootless prey of idleness and depravity."[2] Education without a strong spiritual foundation (focused on wisdom issues) cannot be effective in promoting the human revolution requisite for the transformation from a violent and uncaring to a peaceful and caring civilization. Ikeda maintains:

> I believe that education should be centered on efforts to teach young people that, even when they are removed from the actualities of society, lofty ideals of trust and the courage to respect justice are goals all human beings should aspire to attain.[3]

Without a spiritually enlightened root, education offers no real sustenance to human beings. What Ikeda calls a "flight from learning" is students' rejection of knowledge that fails to meet their deep spiritual needs. When education fails to connect with the greater self and deprives people of spiritual nourishment, it fails to fulfill one of its essential functions.

Curbing the flight from learning involves learning from the wisdom of our predecessors. The accumulated body of wisdom from all humanity represents the cultural mother lode humanity conveys from one generation to the next.

Philosophically based education does not take its lead from government and big business. The function of learning is not to create a better cog for the wheel:

> The educational world today can be said to concern itself solely with producing human resources. In modern society, human beings, like mercenaries in times of war, are only means to an end. Education cultivates people who are useful only to the extent to which they fit into various slots in society.[4]

For Ikeda, "[t]he true goal education should be the cultivation of the individual personality on the basis of respect for humanity."[5] In instances when economic, political, and technical values are considered more valuable than the dignity of the person, learning becomes debased:

> By devoting itself to a utilitarianism that over emphasizes [sic] intellectual knowledge and technological skills, education in modern society has two major bad consequences. First, by making learning a tool of politics and economics, it has robbed learning of its inherent dignity and independence. Second, people engaged in learning and education become the slaves of intellectual knowledge and technological skill, which are the only aspects of learning prized today. As an outcome of this trend, respect for humanity declines. In short, today people are compelled to serve intellectual knowledge and technological skill, which are in turn controlled by politics and economics.[6]

Taught to manipulate and manipulated themselves, students look at the world as theirs to do with as they please. Without dialogue and the inner search for truth, we fail to discover that in order to turn others into objects, we must turn ourselves into objects. Other people cannot become objects of our greed unless we first make ourselves into greedy objects. Suckled on exploitative educational practices promoting greed, we become the purveyors of widespread destruction:

> Modern scientific-technological civilization has given virtually free rein to human greed—it is in fact a product of liberated material greed—and unless all of us perceive this fact with maximum clarity and base our judgments on this perception, we will be unable to stop the destruction of our natural environment and the possible annihilation of mankind.[7]

In contradistinction to scientific-technological education, philosophically based education is a return to a wisdom-oriented educational approach. Wisdom-oriented education sees the inner search for truth as the ultimate value of education. The search for inner truth and the evolution of the spirit toward Buddhahood allows people to see that "the dignity of life must be the basic principle on which all our actions rest."[8]

Seventeen

HOPE AS A MORAL VIRTUE

inertia is darkness, hope is light
retreat is death, advance is life

Daisaku Ikeda
"Song of Building" in *Songs from My Heart*

In "The Cherry Tree," Ikeda tells the tale of the rebirth of hope. Set in a Japanese village during wartime, the story begins on a note of despair:

> Taichi and his sister, Yumiko, lived with their mother in an abandoned farmhouse. Their country had been at war, and airplanes had dropped bombs on their village. Their own house lay in ruins, and their father was dead. For Taichi and Yumiko, the bombs had shattered their world into a thousand pieces. Their mother's heart was shattered too.[1]

While their mother takes the long trek to town each day to work, the children play outside in the ruins. They meet an old man who wraps straw matting around a sickly, "ugly, hobbled" cherry tree that had not blossomed since before the war. He wants to protect the tree from the upcoming winter. The children think it quite dead, but the old man is convinced that the tree would bloom one day, perhaps not in his lifetime but sometime.

Upon the urging of their mother, the children help the old man save the cherry tree, crucial to sheltering wildlife: "It's never hurts to hope," their mother says. During winter, the children brush the snow off the tree's branches. The old man remains convinced the old tree will bloom, but the children remain skeptical. In the spring, the cherry tree comes back to life. It looked like it did before the war. As the tree blossoms, so does the once-devastated village. With the emergence of more economic opportunities, their mother can work in the village instead of walking to town. Like the cherry tree, the family flourishes.

Hope is an attitude toward the world, but attitudes are pre-actions. Pre-actions point us point our direction. This is what Ikeda means when he says: "Hope is not the seed but the sun which shines within the heart of each person."[2] Without that light of hope, we can't see the paths of light. Or perhaps, the paths of life are not even there without hope. The light of hope nurtures expectations and points us toward the future. We can look on the future the same way we look at the present: as an old sickly cherry tree that hasn't bloomed in a while. Or we can imagine what the cherry tree can become.

The blanket of despair covering the village produces inertia. Such inertia contributes to fatalistic beliefs, similar to lowest state of the ten states of being, hell. In the state of hell, we believe everything is as it is and cannot become other than what it is.

Hope is an assertive attitude working on the world. This is what Ikeda suggests when he says: "Hope is not the seed but the sun which shines within the heart of each person." The sun sheds light, but does more than shed light. It helps things grow. Without hopes, we cannot see the paths of possibilities; nor would they even be there. Hope is the light and life of spirit. Hope is an attitude transforming ugly into the beautiful, the ridiculous into the sublime, and the barren into the bountiful.

At the beginning of the story, only the old man, with the very special gift of hope, believes the cherry tree would blossom again. Everybody else believes it is dead. In the same way the old man believes that the cherry tree will blossom again, so Ikeda believes that human ideals will one day flourish:

> Challenge the discord of hope and despair
> all forms of barbarism
> take away the poison from the air
> take away the poison from the water
> take away the poison from the grain
> pluck the evil talons from the atom
> dispel the dark of ignorance from mankind![3]

Rebirth is crucial to hope. We can start over—as many times as necessary. Each moment of our lives can be a rebirth:

> Nothing is hopeless. The worst mistake you can make when young is to give up on a dream, to not challenge yourself for fear of failure. The past is the past and the future is the future. Keep moving forward with a steady on what is ahead, telling yourself: "I'll start from today!" "I'll start fresh from this moment!" This spirit—starting from the present moment—is at the heart of Buddhist philosophy.[4]

There can be false hopes, for example, in the state of Heavenly Beings when we miscalculate our abilities to shape the world. The hope of which Ikeda speaks is the not the deluded hope of the boastful child who believes he can swim though he has had no swimming lessons. The hope of which Ikeda speaks is the heuristic hope that is like a messenger from the future who tells us that what we do now will matter in the future. Without that messenger from the future, the present can only be seen as a sickly cherry tree.

Hope is a moral virtue, perhaps the most important. If our actions matter, they matter because they have some future effects. Without hope, why would anybody care about those effects at all? Without hope, why would care about good and evil? The apathetic, cynical, indifferent, and alienated person could care less about good and evil. The hopeful person cares deeply about "the vital drama of the struggle between good and evil" and is determined that good ultimately triumphs.[5]

Eighteen

TRUST AND HARMONY

Be kind and polite to others, oppose violence, and foster trust and harmony.
School Precept, Soka Schools

In the works of Daisaku Ikeda, trust is encountered in five ways: (1) as the essence of a smoothly running society; (2) as fragile and easily destructible; (3) as a litmus test for progress in nuclear arms contest; (4) as essential to cognition in the absence of reason; and as (5) as an ideal of education.

For Ikeda, "mutual trust makes possible the smooth running of society as a whole." In Plato's *Republic*, for example, the ideal society is described is the one with the most harmony.[1] Different people and organizations cooperate so that the overall result is harmony. Harmony presupposes trust. People can't cooperate unless they trust one another on some level. The harmonious society is the trusting society. When deep levels of distrust exist, especially with respect to nuclear arms, then harmony is hard pressed to exist.

Trust is fragile. It is hard to build up, easy to destroy. Trust is especially easy to destroy because of the lack of solid connections with other people. The most trusting relationships with others are based on compassion. The compassionate person understands why other people do what they do and feels for them. Bathed in light of compassion, other people's intentions are not considered evil. Suspicious and egoistic people, without feeling for others, fail to understand others. Lacking compassion, they see a worm at the core of intentions and actions.

The search for meaning in our lives is the search for what is trustworthy and what is not—what can add value to our lives and what cannot. Technology, Ikeda points out, is not the sole benchmark for progress:

> Now that we no longer accept with unquestioning faith the idea that material progress in beneficial without qualification, we ought to attempt to reevaluate the significance of the very idea of progress and in that way discover to what extent what is worthy of trust.[2]

The oldest and most easily forgotten lesson is that the quest for things makes us things and the possession our humanity makes us human.

Lack of trust is one of the four factors why the arms race has faltered:

> Lack of trust, national egoism, indifference to the danger, and expansion of nonmilitary use of atomic energy—these are the four elements that I believe hinder arms reduction.[3]

The evil of nuclear weapons is not limited to their destructive power. The evil of nuclear power extends to the profound distrust it cultivates. While the mushroom clouds are the overwhelming negative image associated with nuclear weapons, just as insidious are the fissures in trust nuclear weapons create. This represents a cataclysmic destruction of the spirit:

> The evil lies not only in their overwhelming power to cause destruction and death, but also in the profound distrust emanating and growing out of their possession. It is this distrust that has created the so-called cult of deterrence.[4]

When we trust arms, we distrust people. We have weapons because we fear others. The more we trust arms, the less we believe that we can work together for peace; the less we believe in the goodness of human nature and the ideal widespread cooperation and good will:

> Trust in nuclear arms is a negation of trust in humanity. The more people trust in arms, the less they trust each other. Ceasing to put their trust in arms is the only way to cultivate mutual trust among peoples.[5]

The more trust in the world, the more value: "relations of trust lead to agreements connected with the creation of value."[6] The more people enrich one another on multiple levels (economic, spiritual, aesthetic, moral), the more value brought into the world.

Trust operates at heart of our every-day experience of the world. An over-trust in reason sometimes clouds our vision of the future:

> But, no matter how polished, refined, and strengthened, reason properly operates in situations like the one mentioned above [as a means of preventing mistakes]; and, as human beings, we must constantly enter domains that inaccessible to reason: the future toward which the present life is always striving.[7]

Ikeda marks out the limits of reason, and the future is inaccessible to reason. The future is accessible only to the strongest form of trust, faith. Though we search for the cold hard facts of reason, we often place our trust in premonitions, intuitions, and the ideas of other people because of we are limited in knowledge:

> Of course, the relatively constant laws operative in various phenomena make possible a certain amount of forecasting on the basis of rational investigation into the past. Since it is impossible for an individual to have rational understanding of all phenomena, however, it is sometimes necessary to attempt to cope with the future by believing in elucidations made by other people. People who are ignorant or untutored in teachings from the past must use their own premonitions and intuitions as guides to the future. Under such circumstances, .we must put faith in our premonitions and intuition just as in daily life we must put faith in information received from our eyes and ears.[8]

Trust is one of the most important ideals of higher education. The codification of trust can erode the need for weapons and illuminate the bounds of reason. When we have properly identified what is worthy of trust, we then can work towards harmony.

Nineteen

FAITH AND ULTIMATE MEANING

The ultimate law
wherein join those distant paths,
which mingles this dimension of the life within me
to the unending movements of the universe,
this I make my faith

Daisaku Ikeda
"A Believer" in *Songs from My Heart*

Faith cannot be eradicated. In the human condition faith can be transferred from one account to another, but no matter how many times transferred it remains faith. Even the most disciplined skeptics must admit they have faith that their theories are true, for it they didn't what value would their theories have? Faith can be of mundane or profound matters. Faith in our abilities and faith that others will keep their promises are instances of faith in the smaller sense. In the profound sense, faith refers to the most important task for spiritual beings—creating meaning:

The formula for the enrichment of human nature—
it exists nowhere but in
A complete and all-embracing faith
The profound search for a meaningful life –
It exists
in a faith that is lofty[1]

"Faith is an open mind, a pure heart and a flexible spirit" is one of Ikeda's primary messages. Faith is not the product of rejecting doubt, but is the result of ultimate inquiry. Faith is reserved for those matters that reason cannot reach.

In an age of science and technology, faith appears antiquarian. The rejection of religion is often followed by the creation of belief systems that are not called religions, but rest on faith. Faith in material success and science are religions:

> If religion is interpreted in the conventional sense modern western civilization seems to have arisen as an outcome of the very act of rejecting religion. But in another light the modern world has its own kinds of religion founded on aspirations for material success and faith in scientific progress.[2]

According to Ikeda, humans are to seek "a new balance between faith in ourselves and recognition of a power that is greater than we are."[3]

The newer "religions" of scientific progress, nationalism, and communism cultivate greed, whereas the older religions seek to eliminate greed:

> I sense one common point distinguishing the new religions—faith in scientific progress, nationalism, and communism—from such older ones as Christianity, Buddhism, and Islam. Whereas the older religions strove to control and suppress human greed, the new ones seem to have originated—at least to be employed—for the sake of the liberation of fulfillment of that greed. I consider this to be the basic nature of the new religions, and in that nature I see the fundamental problem facing all three of them.[4]

Materialistic religions develop the lesser self, whereas the traditional religions develop the greater self. The lesser self practices faith in the smaller sense: faith in our abilities to procure material things. The greater self practices faith in the larger: faith in the search of meaning in life.

Faith "must be the basis of all individual practical activities."[5] It "must be the source of all creative cultural activities" and "must inspire actions in real society."[6] As a true believer in dialogue, Ikeda declares that faith is not immune from the questioning of doubting Thomases: "Though doubt runs counter to faith, this does not mean that one should not doubt. Faith is made deeper and stronger by being subjected to questioning."[7] At the same time, Ikeda contends: "The True Law is beyond all doubting."[8]

For Ikeda, the true law is the Nam-myoho-renge-kyo, the chanting of which fuses us with cosmic life forces. Aware of the 3,000 worlds (*ichinen sanzen*), we compassionately connect with the great wellspring of life:

> Buddhism, which views the whole, incalculable entity of life in terms of the doctrines of the Perfect Teaching and of ichinen sanzen, is the ultimate, eternal religion, opening a path of unquestionable faith that deals not with a conceptual supernatural deity, but with life as we all know and experience it.[9]

With statements such as "opening a path of unquestionable faith," "The True Law is beyond all doubting," and "The ideal for the future must originate from religious faith deep in the human heart," Ikeda can be seen elevating religion to a higher level of philosophy. Saying that any belief is immune to scrutiny can be construed as anti-philosophical. Another way of looking at this issue is to say that while people fused with the life force are immune from doubt, from another perspective, philosophical inquiries can doubt the actuality of the experience.

A larger issue concerns the absence of doubt in enlightenment. The absence of doubt in enlightenment suggests a divine and not a human perspective. Without doubt, why seek the truth? Doubt motivates us to seek truth. If the enlightened ones are not seekers of truth, then can they truly be considered enlightened? How can there be an unshakable foundation and doubt at the same time?

Ikeda describes faith beyond doubt in the following manner:

> The truly firm faith in Buddhism rejects irrationality and agrees with reason in the judgment of those matters which reason is capable of judging. This kind of faith can become the unshakable foundation of all thought and activity.[10]

The foundation is doubt-free not because it is immune from doubts; it is doubt-free because after arduous inquiry, it has been discovered no doubts can affect it. The search for truth always brings the searcher back to the same unshakable foundation.

Twenty

THE SUPERRATIONAL

> The eye of reason is able to see only the waves on the surface of the great sea of the universal force of life. Below lie the immense, incalculable regions of the subconscious, which not irrational but superrational. We should not reject these regions just because they are beyond the reach of reason. It is in this superrational region that the vast energy spurring human beings to think and act is found.
>
> Daisaku Ikeda
> *A Lasting Peace, Volume 2*

The belief in superrational distinguishes Ikeda's new humanism from the predominantly scientifically driven humanism of the twentieth century. For twentieth century humanism, everything can be explained rationally. Knowledge comes in one flavor: rational. Other forms of experience (intuitions, subconscious thoughts) have no status independent of reason. These forms of experience cannot be considered knowledge. They are merely facets of human experience, sideshows to the only real show in town—reason.

Some spheres of knowledge are inaccessible to reason. The dominance of reason is limited. "Reason is clearly incapable of controlling all the phenomena of the force of life. Love, hate, happiness, anger, sorrow, and joy are all beyond its control."[1] The physical aspect of human beings (the body) is the appropriate domain for rational dissection, but the spiritual aspect is outside the province of reason. The Buddhist concept of *Shikishin Funi* demonstrates the twofold distinction:

> the relationship between body and spirit is best expressed in the Buddhist concept of *Shikishin Funi*. The word *shiki* represents all phenomena of life that can be understood by means of scientific or physiochemical methods of research. In other words, *skiki* is the material, or phenomenal, aspect of life. *Shin* refers to all of the various noumenal aspects of life and the many kinds of spiritual activities that cannot be grasped in terms of physiochemical methods. Included in *shin* are reason, intellect, and desires that are the object of investigation by spiritualists. In Buddhist teachings these aspects are at the same time separate and limited.[2]

Spiritual activities are superrational. They cannot be reduced to the processes of the body. Ikeda's new humanism offers independence of the spirit from the body. It also makes reason and intuition partners in knowledge:

> Reason and intuition complement each other in that reason presupposes the function of intuition, while intuition is rectified and clarified by reason. The repeated functioning of the faculty of reason can systematize and elucidate wisdom acquired through intuition. Whereas reason generally adopts the analytic approach and resolves complicated subjects into simple constituent elements, intuition grasps a subject as a whole and penetrates directly to its essential nature.[3]

The act of intuition, of "getting it," is a common human experience, but also a spiritual experience. It transcends neurons and physicality.

Reason is often portrayed as the saint; instincts the sinner. Sometimes reason and instincts are bedfellows. When reason becomes attached to the instincts, it can disrupt harmony, for example, the instinct to dominate is embedded in a moral or legal code. Instead of random instinctive acts, the act becomes institutionalized:

> Though it is frequently spoken of as the opposite of instinct, in my opinion, human reason often destroys the harmony that in nonhuman animals is preserved at various stages of development. In other words, instead of being their opposite, reason works in conjunction with various instinctive elements and, by causing them to amplify to extremes, in either good or bad directions, disrupts harmony. We must, therefore, concern ourselves not with the distinction between reason and instinct, but with the nature of the force stimulating the amplification of the two in conjunction. The fundamental issue is whether the force is one of insecurity and fear or one of hope and kindness.[4]

From this perspective, there is no such thing as a purely intellectual matter. Reason does not rule all and is intertwined with instinct and emotion. Superrational morality is based on this insight:

> Morality is generally thought of as the way to control one's innate evil. However, it tends to be an intellectual matter, and human evils involve emotion more often than reason. I believe that religion, which delves deeper into human life than the rational mind, must be the source of the inner strength to control evil and facilitate life on a high moral and ethical plane.[5]

Twentieth-century scientifically driven humanism errs by its rationalistic reductionism. Humanism of this sort wanted to sever the tie between religion and science. Science is considered rational; religion spiritual. Science and religion aren't related at all. But that attitude has shifted as the hubris of science falls in the face of revolutionary discoveries (chaos theory) that undermine apparently impregnable worldviews. In *Quarks, Chaos, and Christianity*, John Polkinghorne suggests that science and religion are related:

> I believe that science and religion are intellectual cousins under the skin. Both are searching for motivated belief. Neither can claim absolutely certain knowledge, for each must base its conclusions on an interplay between interpretation and experience. In consequence, both must be open to the possibility of correction. Neither deals with pure fact, or with mere opinion. They are both part of the great human endeavour to understand.[6]

Ikeda's new superrational humanism complements new scientific worldviews much better than twentieth century empirically driven humanism. The new humanism is richer by its inclusion of nonrational experiences as forms of knowledge. In the final analysis, "reason is not always deserving of the extensive trust. As a matter of fact, the idea that everything can be rationally investigated and judged flies in the face of reality."[7]

PART THREE

IMAGINARY DIALOGUES

Author's Note: In the following ten chapters, I have created imaginary dialogues between Daisaku Ikeda and prominent thinkers. The assumptions are my own, but I have attempted to remain true to the spirit of each thinker's perspective, much as Plato probably did in his dialogues.

Twenty-One

LAO TZU'S HIERARCHY OF EFFECTIVE LEADERSHIP

IKEDA: One of the most intriguing passages in the *Tao The King* is your description of leadership. You begin by saying: "The most intelligent leaders bring about results without making those controlled realize they are being influenced."[1]

LAO TZU: The more subtle leaders barely leave any traces of their influence. The less subtle leaders leave fingerprints of their influence everywhere. It's like comparing two plays having actors fly around the stage. In one the wires are clearly seen; in the other, they are practically invisible.

IKEDA: My distinction between hard and soft power exemplifies your point. Hard power, like military power, is not subtle—one country dominating another by bombs, tanks, and bullets. Soft power is much more subtle kind of influence. Influence through dialogue and cultural exchanges are what I understand soft power to be.

LAO TZU: Less intelligent leaders motivate others in less subtle ways. Awards are a good way to motivate others. Other people are motivated by bonuses or promotions. Some are motivated by flattery. Others can be motivated by loyalty, for example, nationalism.

IKEDA: But for you there are other kinds of motivation that are even less subtle than the ones you just described. You contend: "Those still less intelligent employ fear by making their followers think they will not receive their rewards."

LAO TZU: Scare tactics.

IKEDA: Such leaders probably use the behaviorist stimulus-response method to influence people. But motivating people by fear isn't the worst kind of leadership.

LAO TZU: The least subtle leadership consists of trying to improve others by condemning their conduct.

IKEDA: Preaching at them.

LAO TZU: Exactly.

IKEDA: Once you have finished describing the four kinds of leadership, you state:

> But since, if leaders do not trust their followers then their followers will not trust their leaders.
>
> The intelligent leader will be careful not to speak as if he doubted or distrusted his follower's ability to do the job suitably.[2]

My question for you is this: Does the last statement refer only to the worst kind of leadership or all three of the less subtle forms of leadership?

LAO TZU: That's something my interpreters must decide.

IKEDA: Let me give it a try then. Moral condemnation may motivate a person on a short-term basis, but it isn't going to forge a trusting relationship between leaders and followers. When leaders morally condemn their followers, their followers can easily interpret this as a sign of mistrust. As you suggest, trust builds trust; mistrust builds mistrust. Mistrustful leadership begets mistrustful followers.

LAO TZU: That is an interesting interpretation.

IKEDA: Let me take this further. Motivating people by fear also creates distrust. It tells the follower: "You are not capable unless I hang a reward over your head. You will not accomplish your tasks without being threatened." That certainly isn't trusting.

LAO TZU: No, it isn't.

IKEDA: Appeals to loyalty, flattery, honor, and self-interest also exhibit a lack of trust in followers. If I believe that my followers won't complete their tasks without some kind of an award, then I suggest to them that they can be bought and that they are not intelligent enough to understand they have been bought. I hardly think this builds mistrust, but it does not serve to create trust.

LAO TZU: I wonder how you would respond to my final statement in that section: "When the work is done, and as he [the leader] wanted it done, he will be happy if the followers say: 'This is just the way we wanted it.'"[3]

IKEDA: A sure sign of subtle leadership is that the task is completed as the leader wants and as the subject wants it. But I would argue that this is not because of some kind of mind control on the part of leaders, but something else.

LAO TZU: I never say what it is.

IKEDA: You never do, but I believe I can come up with a plausible answer. One option is that the more subtle leaders clearly know the needs, abilities, and objectives of their followers and design activities that reflect those needs, abilities, and objectives. Another option is that the subtle leaders have created deep level of trust between their followers and themselves and that creates a sense of community. When community is felt by, tasks are not individual deeds, but group deeds, things that "we" desire.

LAO TZU: You have a good imagination.

IKEDA: Your typology of leaders can certainly be applied to the classroom. Trust must be built up in the classroom between teachers and students. The teacher can't come at students like grand inquisitors. Nor can the teacher act like deities who if not worshipped will take away their followers' rewards. Nor can teachers act like game show hosts, promising contestants fortunes.

LAO TZU: I don't know what a game show host is, but they don't sound subtle.

IKEDA: In the ideal classroom, teachers trust their students to exercise self-control. Thus I would suggest that the subtlest form of leadership is based on the assumption of the followers exercising self-control, achieving self-mastery That is a profound gesture of trust.

Twenty-Two

PLATO'S NOTION OF MASS ENLIGHTENMENT

IKEDA: Thank you for making the long trip to Japan.
PLATO: I am honored to be here. The green tea is excellent. Do you mind if I take some back to Socrates?
IKEDA: Not at all. Your philosophy is so rich I could start off anywhere. But I would like to begin with your idea of enlightenment. In the *Republic*, you suggest that only a certain group of persons can be enlightened: those with "gold souls." Only people with gold souls possess the wisdom to rule, to become philosopher-kings or philosopher-queens.[1] From my perspective, mass enlightenment is possible.
PLATO: People obviously have different innate abilities and different gifts. Only a few people are gifted with wisdom. Those few have the potential to become the rulers of the control.
IKEDA: Like Nichiren Daishonin, I contend all beings can be enlightened. The spark is in everybody. Wisdom is not limited to a few people, the ruling class of your ideal state.
PLATO: That is one of the fundamental differences in your thinking and mine. You have a stubborn egalitarian streak in you, while I embrace an aristocratic perspective. When egalitarians look at the question of innate knowledge, they tend to believe everybody has the potential to do anything. From my perspective, only a few people have the gift. This justifies why governments should be run by a small group of wise people.

A harmonious society is based on people doing what they do best. People who bake best become bakers; people who fight best become soldiers; people who think best become philosophers. The ones who think best are best suited for running the society.

IKEDA: Thinking best means thinking rationally.
PLATO: That is my view. Rationality is the basis for discovering truth.
IKEDA: You assume that the most rational should run the society?
PLATO: That is my assumption, sir.
IKEDA: Rationality has its limits, Plato. It cannot connect us with underlying reality.
PLATO: Why not?
IKEDA: From my perspective, reason can dissect and analyze things. Underlying reality cannot simply be grasped with the intellect. It can only be grasped by compassionate intellect. Only by developing the gifts of compassion and reason can human beings grasp the greater unity—unity with other people and with the universe.

PLATO: Compassionate wisdom?
IKEDA: Rationality can posit connectedness, but it can't feel it. The feeling of connectedness is essential to grasping underlying reality. Your philosopher-kings and philosopher-queens are not necessarily the wisest of people. The wisest of people are gifted rationally and compassionately. Reason by itself cannot lead people to enlightenment.
PLATO: But this does not undercut my argument that only a small number of people possess the gift of wisdom.
IKEDA: Even if I assume as you do that a minority possesses the gift of compassionate wisdom, I do not know *a priori* who has this gift and when it will emerge. If I can't say who has the gift, I must begin with premise that everybody has it until proven wrong.
PLATO: That's extremely messy. If you go with my noble lie of people being born gold, silver, and bronze souls, then you can neatly place people in each group and educate them appropriately.
IKEDA: You're prejudging.
PLATO: If we breed the bright people with the bright people, we're going to produce bright people, people with gold souls. And if by chance someone shows potential in any of the other classes in society, that person can become part of the gold class.
IKEDA: The profound compassion of Nichiren Buddhism compels us to enlighten others. That is the mission of the enlightened.
PLATO: You can't believe that everybody will be enlightened. That strikes me as entirely unrealistic.
IKEDA: All beings can be enlightened.
PLATO: Mass enlightenment is a foreign concept to me.
IKEDA: I am not so sure you mean that. In your famous parable of the cave, the philosophers who escape the cave and grasp the truth return to the cave.[2] Why do they return? They want to enlighten others and perhaps are motivated by their compassion. Even within your aristocratic viewpoint, Plato, is the possibility for the enlightenment and liberation of all.
PLATO: Reason, then, is not the be-all and end-all of education
IKEDA: Plato, when you use the beautiful image of the philosopher as a midwife helping people give birth to their ideas, I couldn't agree more. But the ideas that people give birth to superrational ideas. Potentially, they contain Buddhahood within them.
PLATO: The superrational?
IKEDA: Educators need to move beyond your image of reason steering the passions and appetites. Reason can never tell us what is right or wrong. Only compassion can and that's part of the superrational. The greatest compassion can only emerge when we grasp the whole, grasp it with the full spectrum of intelligence, reason and compassion. Only when we use the eye of Buddha can we discern ultimate reality.
PLATO: Mass enlightenment is far-fetched.

IKEDA: From the perspective of Buddha, it is not. It is just beyond the next mountain. And if not that one, the next. Or the next. Or the next. But somewhere, it is.

Twenty-Three

JOHN STUART MILL'S HIGHER AND LOWER PLEASURES

IKEDA: I am struck by your distinction between higher and lower pleasures. In your essay *Utilitarianism*, you say that it is better to be Socrates dissatisfied than a pig satisfied.[1]

MILL: Human happiness is much more complex than satisfying physical urges. We require intellectual fulfillment as well. Even if we don't reach intellectual fulfillment, striving for them enriches our lives.

IKEDA: Do people know the difference between higher and lower pleasures?

MILL: Yes. But people who have not experienced higher pleasures cannot really judge what is what.

IKEDA: I relate what you say about higher and lower pleasures to the distinction between the lesser and greater self. The lesser self seeks the lower pleasures of which you speak—materialistic and sensual pursuits. The greater self seeks the higher pleasures involved connecting with the life force of the universe.

MILL: Lately, I have been dissatisfied with my distinction between higher and lower pleasures. There seems to be something missing.

IKEDA: I have a suggestion for reformulating your distinction, possibly enriching it. Would you be offended?

MILL: No, not at all.

IKEDA: Are you familiar with the ten states of being?

MILL: A little.

IKEDA: The ten states of being illuminate the evolution of human spirituality. These states include, from least to most evolved: hell, hungry spirits, animals, warlike demons, humanity, heavenly beings, voice hearers, cause-awakened ones, bodhisattvas, and Buddhas or enlightened ones. These provide a benchmark for evaluating human spiritual growth and helping us make the distinction between higher and lower pleasures.

MILL: The lower pleasures are hell, hungry spirits, animals, and war-like demons?

IKEDA: Correct. They are the four evil paths. The pleasures of these states are short-lived, self-destructive, and ultimately unfulfilling. The despair and feelings of helplessness in hell can only be described as self-torture. In the state of hungry spirits, the desire to devour is never satisfied. In the state of animals, relying on instinct only can get us in trouble. And in the state of war-like demons, we feel large and important as we experience hatred, but that feeling of looming large is as temporary as the anger.

MILL: The lower pleasures correspond to the four evil paths.
IKEDA: That is correct.
MILL: And the other six states represent the higher pleasures.
IKEDA: I wouldn't go that far. The state of humanity may be in the twilight zone between higher and lower pleasures. From the tranquility in the state of humanity, we can ascend toward Buddhahood and be pulled down into the four evils.
MILL: What about those in the states of heavenly beings, voice-hearers, and cause-awakened ones?
IKEDA: These states are more disposed toward higher pleasure, but like the stock market can tumble. They are still connected to the material world. In the compassionate state of bodhisattvas and Buddhas, which are characterized by internal welling up of life force, the pure higher pleasures can be experienced.
IKEDA: The experience of higher pleasures offers a different sense of time and space. Those experiencing lower pleasures regard space as nothing more than their physical bodies and senses. Those experiencing higher pleasures have a much different view of space. They feel themselves in different parts of space, have a sense of ubiquity. I would say that one of the signs of the experience of higher pleasures, what we might call an elevated feeling, is a feeling of ubiquity. The spatial experience is not limited to bodily sensations, but to the imagination, the spirit transcending one point in space.
MILL: How does the experience of higher pleasure affect the experience of time?
IKEDA: In the lower pleasures, life-time, the way we experience time, is perceived to move more slowly than time as we conventionally measure it, in seconds, minutes, days, years, etc. In the state of hell, for example, one minute of measured time feels like an eternity. Time passes excruciatingly slowly. On the other side of the spectrum, time rapidly passes in the higher states of being. In the higher states, people can live thousands of lifetimes with the passing of measured time. Life experience is so rich and fulfilling in the higher states that everything rushes by us.
MILL: Before I talk about time, let me review space. The closer we approach Buddhahood, the more space expands for us. The expansion of space gives us a sense of ubiquity, of feeling like we are everywhere and connected with everything.
IKEDA: That is an interesting way of putting it.
MILL: From a temporal perspective, the closer we approach Buddhahood the more quickly we perceive time to be flowing. In the higher pleasures, the flow of time is faster than the lower pleasures.

IKEDA: The higher the pleasure the more fused we are to the universal life force. This compassionate fusion is the essence of Buddahood.
MILL: The expansion of space and the rapidity of time experience constitute are the essence of the higher values. That is an exciting discovery.
IKEDA: Intellectual fulfillment redefines spiritual space and time coordinates as we know them.

Twenty-Four

ALFRED NORTH WHITEHEAD'S INERT IDEAS

IKEDA: If anything kills student initiative more quickly in education than boredom, I don't know what it is. Being "bored to death" comes pretty close to the truth. Your concept of inert ideas explains at least one facet of student boredom.

WHITEHEAD: Ideas can be the lifeblood of human activity. They can spur human beings to fall in the love, as great dramas do, or even give up their lives, as great speeches do. Yet, they can also put us to sleep. Inert ideas are sleeping pills, and when slipped to students you might as well have toothpicks at every desk so students can keep their eyes open.

IKEDA: How do inert ideas cause boredom?

WHITEHEAD: They cause boredom because in the language people use today students don't "connect" with them. Another way to put it is that students don't think the ideas have any relevance.

IKEDA: Is it the ideas themselves that are irrelevant or something else?

WHITEHEAD: It is less than ideas themselves and more what the mind does with ideas.

IKEDA: This is what you mean by "dead knowledge"?

WHITEHEAD: Yes. Dead knowledge consists of inert ideas.[1] Ideas become inert when they are simply received by the mind. If the mind is active—if it tests ideas, if it creates new ideas by combining several notions, if it evaluates ideas—the fossilization of ideas will not occur. When the mind is passive, the ideas it receives will sit there, atrophy, and exude rigor mortis.

IKEDA: From your perspective, the mind is inherently active. Yet schooling can transform the most active, creative mind into a passive dump of inert ideas. What is the source of inert ideas?

WHITEHEAD: The rote memorization of book learning is the primary source of inert. Students are isolated from the ideas that motivate them.

IKEDA: I assume you mean: "There is only one subject-matter for education, and that is Life in all its manifestations."[2]

WHITEHEAD: Unless education is entangled with the lives of students, I predict inert ideas will be predominant.

IKEDA: Value creation is central to my educational pedagogy and my ethical and political philosophy in general. The more positive values we bring into the world, the more meaning our lives have. You contend that that rote memorization and similar techniques less our appreciation of diverse values in the environment.

WHITEHEAD: That is true, but I would like to add another dimension to the discussion of value.
IKEDA: Please go on.
WHITEHEAD: These values are not the values of the scholar or the practical person calculating the worth of something in the marketplace. These are the values of ordinary persons aesthetically attuned to their environments.
IKEDA: Your concept of inert ideas is a rich vein for further inquiry. We can say that for traditional schooling, scientific reasoning is considered the highest activity.
WHITEHEAD: Yes.
IKEDA: The highest kind of reasoning is also the most disconnected from life and the wide array of values of which you speak. In order to grasp "life in all of its manifestations," students must have discovered a connection with life, not simply from the perspective of theories and abstractions. I believe your fight against inert ideas is really a fight to cultivate another way of knowing in students.
WHITEHEAD: Are you referring to superrational thinking?
IKEDA: Precisely. Superrational thinking encompasses reason, compassion, intuition, all states of knowing. Another of your famous sayings is that education should become "a seamless coat of learning."[3] What I understand by this phrase is that our experience of schooling should not be disconnected, discrete facts in different nooks and grannies. Our experience of schooling should be flowing and interconnected, as information, knowledge, and wisdom form a meaningful whole.
WHITEHEAD: We cannot grasp life in its manifestations unless the present bent of abstraction is replaced with something more holistic, what you call the superrational.
IKEDA: That is my point. As I recently said to Plato, the superrational is our true connection with ultimate ground of our being.
WHITEHEAD: That sounds too spiritual to me.
IKEDA: The superrational is the spiritual aspect of human beings. "Life in all of its manifestations" includes the spiritual.
WHITEHEAD: I suppose so.
IKEDA: Holism is an empty concept without referring to the superrational and our spirituality. Our spiritual attunement to reality provides us with a picture of reality as a seamless coat, as you say. The seamless coat of learning in education is hardly possible when people look at reality in a fragmented way. The seamless coat of education is possible to the extent that people can view the universe as a seamless coat.
WHITEHEAD: In order seamless coat of education to exist, there must first be a seamless coat of reality.

IKEDA: Once we cultivate the higher states of being, the higher values as John Stuart Mill what say, the seamless coat of education may be possible.

Twenty-Five

JOHN DEWEY'S PARTICIPATORY EDUCATION

IKEDA: Alfred North Whitehead identifies "inert ideas" as a fundamental danger to schooling. When schooling fails to connect with "life in all its manifestations," then inert ideas or dead knowledge is the result.
DEWEY: I agree with Whitehead that the actual experience of the student is thc most important. I see this actual experience as the acquisition of symbols and not as sudden gushing of natural abilities. Only by participating in social situations can students learn about symbols. Using Whitehead's language, inert ideas can be avoided when students tackle real-life problems.
IKEDA: Like Whitehead, you assume that the mind is naturally active.
DEWEY: Yes. Educators don't make children participants; they are naturally participants. Thus the one goal of education is to make education possible, to create a cultural environment in which human beings can grow. Teachers channel the naturally participatory nature toward socially desirable ends.
IKEDA: One of the biggest challenges we have in contemporary education is to foster global awareness in students. As the elbowroom between people becomes less and less and different human beings and cultures regularly intermingle not only on the existential level but also through the media (especially the internet), tolerance and understanding become the leading values of schooling.
DEWEY: Tolerance and understanding are unlikely to emerge from education that inculcates or education that aimlessly wanders. In my *Philosophy of Education*, I posit an intermediary between two:

> The alternative is the kind of education that connects the materials and methods an methods by which knowledge is acquired with a sense of how thing are done and of how they might be done; not by impregnating the individual with some final philosophy, whether it be from Karl Marx, or from Mussolini or Hitler or anybody else, but by enabling him to so understand existing conditions that an attitude of intelligent action will follow from social understanding.[1]

IKEDA: In principle, I support the intermediary position of which you speak. A "hands on" approach to education offers students opportunities to connect with their communities improves and deepens their learning. Yet I believe you neglect a crucial aspect.
DEWEY: And that is?

IKEDA: The idea of human revolution. Human beings have the spark within to dramatically change themselves. While you contend that human beings have naturally active minds and have a natural desire to participate, I am saying something much stronger. I am saying human beings have the ability to dramatically change their spiritual lives.
DEWEY: Participation hinges on individuals becoming cultural beings, which depends upon social-symbolic experience.
IKEDA: I see a deeper level of participation on the spiritual level. When people turn inward and discover the life force within them, they will be able to participate in a much broader manner than you imagine.
DEWEY: How so?
IKEDA: There is no greater participation than a feeling of unity with the underlying life force. In this way, human beings feel connected with all things in the universe.
DEWEY: What about the quantity of shared experiences and the intensity of discussions about them?
IKEDA: This approach has some shortcomings. For example, these shared experiences and the intensity of discussions can only occur in a specific time and specific place among specific people.
DEWEY: And your point is?
IKEDA: My point is this approach is extremely limited. Small groups of people (if we're lucky) can share experiences and intense discussions about these shared experiences can ensue. While this approach brings people together, it can never extend to a universal level. It is highly implausible for highly diverse groups and individuals all over the world to share common experiences on a regular basis, except perhaps via the mass media. On the other hand, people can feel unity with other people and everything in the universe by searching within.
DEWEY: You see my approach as impractical and ineffective.
IKEDA: Not ineffective, but incomplete. Building community begins with building the self. Until people recognize the larger sense of sense, the greater self, then building community becomes problematic. Community outreach is implausible if people lack the compassion to reach out.
DEWEY: You're talking about the creation of a spiritual community emerging by people tapping into their spirituality and becoming enlightened.
IKEDA: I am. But what I mean by enlightenment cannot be divorced from the idea of the enlightened helping other people achieve enlightenment.
DEWEY: The enlightened feel compelled to help others?
IKEDA: The enlightened feel compelled, but not by environmental factors. The most enlightened are the most compassionate. Spurred on by compassion, the enlightened want to bring enlightenment to all people and all being in the universe.

DEWEY: I will give you this: your concept of participation is much broader than what I propose. But I would argue that your concept is a philosophical abstraction that cannot be empirically verified.

IKEDA: A multi-faceted understanding of the mind allows for a multi-dimensional perspective of reality. It allows for spirituality and the global connectedness so desperately needed in this age. The global dialogue I advocate cannot take place unless human beings are ready to be connected.

Twenty-Six

ANTONIO GRAMSCI'S ORGANIC INTELLECTUAL

IKEDA: One of the major principles of Nichiren Daishonin's Buddhism is that all people have the capacity to be enlightened. For you, all human activities contain the germ of intellectualism. Every person has a view of the world and some conception of a moral code. One of the major principles of your political and social philosophy and educational theory is that while all human beings are intellectuals, not all people function as intellectuals.[1] What do you mean by that?

GRAMSCI: Have you ever cooked a meal or hammered in a nail?

IKEDA: Of course.

GRAMSCI: Does that make you cook and a carpenter?

IKEDA: No.

GRAMSCI: You can cook and hammer in a nail (you have the ability to do so), but that is not your social function. While all people can think, not all serve the societal function as intellectuals.

IKEDA: From your perspective, intellectuals, a group including managers, civil servants, clergy, professors, teachers, technicians, and scientists, bind each social group together. Intellectuals are do magically grow outside a social class. They emerge from and serve a social class. For example, if the ruling class of a country decides to militarize, it will fund those intellectuals who support that cause. Pacifist groups will utilize its intellectuals in a much different way.

GRAMSCI: That is correct. Intellectuals are not a distinct social category. They are born within specific classes.

IKEDA: Intellectuals appear to be an independent class, but that is usually a myth. You identify two kinds of intellectuals: traditional intellectuals and organic intellectuals.

GRAMSCI: Traditional intellectuals, no matter how much they consider themselves to be autonomous, are allied with the ruling class. Philosophers, writers, and clergy are prime examples of traditional intellectuals. Organic intellectuals do not play at being independent. The ruling class manufactures these intellectuals for the purpose of maintaining its dominance.

IKEDA: Intellectuals play a huge role in creating a new form of consciousness, for you, a socialist consciousness that can transform society.

GRAMSCI: I see intellectuals as active participants in everyday life. They simply don't give pretty speeches, but get their hands dirty. They are constructors, organizers, and "permanent persuaders" of society. The working

class grows its own organic intellectuals, who along with a select group of traditional intellectuals, bring about revolutionary activity.
IKEDA: I am not as pessimistic as you are about intellectuals who stand against the dominant group. I think we need to introduce a third group of intellectuals who are neither organic nor traditional.
GRAMSCI: And what would they be?
IKEDA: They have to be intellectuals who are prepared to participate in a global world. They might be called diasporic intellectuals. These intellectuals should be thought of as links between different groups, as mediators, rather than pushing the agenda of one group.
GRAMSCI: But these intellectuals still perform a service: to bridge difference and promote understanding. That is an ideology. They still have an agenda.
IKEDA: Yes, I can see that.
GRAMSCI: And I would be willing to say that such intellectuals are not independent forces, but are marshaled by some group or alliance of groups, whether those be Amnesty International, Greenpeace, or other groups.
IKEDA: There is another possibility.
GRAMSCI: Which is?
IKEDA: The intellectual in the image of Buddha: the compassionate intellectual.
GRAMSCI: Why is compassion so important?
IKEDA: Compassion transcends self, nation, and even species. Compassion takes us everywhere. Compassion is not simply imagination. Compassion is empathetic and sympathetic imagination. Compassion transcends spiritual boundaries.
GRAMSCI: Where are you going with this?
IKEDA: The diasporic intellectual has an allegiance to compassion.
GRAMSCI: I would argue that the diasporic intellectual is not an independent group, but as you said, the image of Buddha, which would suggest to me a relationship with Buddhist organization such as your own.
IKEDA: I am not denying there are such creatures, but the diasporic intellectuals I have in mind are people who have had spiritual revolutions and have become Buddha-like.
GRAMSCI: Your criteria for evaluating who is or isn't Buddha-like derives from Buddhist ideology. Buddhism desires to create as many Buddhists as possible to increase its political scope. Thus it defines standards of intelligence to develop organic intellectuals who will strengthen its organization. In order for a technological society to flourish, intelligence will be measured in terms of mathematical and scientific aptitude. In a technological society, mathematical and scientific aptitude is considered the highest form of intelligence because such intellectuals are required to perpetuate that form of life. Since the Buddhist society and its perpetuation is not based on mathematical and technological aptitude, then they will not be deemed the highest forms of intelligence. Instead, compassionate wisdom will be.

IKEDA: I see your point, but I must still insist that even if Buddhism seeks to perpetuate itself, that does not mean there isn't the compassionate intellectual of which I spoke. The compassionate intellectual can be the person of conscience, who follows the heart and mind and is willing to have no allegiance except to the truth.

Twenty-Seven

MARTIN LUTHER KING, JR.'S TOUGH-MINDEDNESS AND TENDER-HEARTEDNESS

IKEDA: In *The Strength to Love*, you describe the ideal thinker: one who is tough-minded and tenderhearted. A balance between these opposites is difficult to achieve. Idealists are rarely realistic; the humble are rarely self-assertive; the militant are rarely passive and the passive are rarely militant.
KING: The tough-minded and tenderhearted thinker is similar to Buddhahood. Compassion compels us to change the world, but only a strong heart, not a bleeding one, has the fortitude to change social evils.
IKEDA: Buddhahood is characterized by the fusion of wisdom and compassion.
KING: Before speaking about the ideal, we best make some initial distinctions: tough-mindedness versus soft-mindedness and tenderheartedness versus hardheartedness.
IKEDA: With respect to soft-mindedness, you assert that gullibility and superstition are hallmarks of soft-mindedness.
KING: Fear of change is a more subtle aspect of soft-mindedness.
IKEDA: You have a wonderful passage where you hit fear of change right on the head:

> The softminded [sic] man always fears change. He feels security in the status quo, and he has almost a morbid fear of the new. For him, the greatest pain in the pain of the new idea. . . . The softminded person always wants to freeze the moment and hold life in the gripping yoke of sameness.[1]

KING: Soft-minded people find a refuge in security. Following the same routines and the same customs becomes a security blanket for the soft-minded. Security is their greatest pleasure. The secure world for them is the world frozen in time, where everything stays the same.
IKEDA: This is why the new unsettles the soft-minded. The new is different and the soft-minded are confounded by anything outside what they know.
KING: On the political and social level, soft-minded people living in an unjust system are hardly the best catalysts to bring about change.
IKEDA: Soft-minded people prejudge instead of postjudging. You don't say this in the essay, but I would say that postjudging is a hardship for those accustomed to security. The ready-made answer is the most secure and doesn't

involve changing the mind. I find a connection between soft-mindedness and what Whitehead describes as inert ideas. The soft-minded embrace inert ideas; the deader the better. Inert ideas do not spark change, but keep everything in the same order. On the other hand, you say

> the tough mind is sharp and penetrating, breaking the crust of legends and myths and sifting the true from the false. The tough-minded individual is astute and discerning. He has a strong, austere quality that makes for firmness of purpose and solidness of commitment.[2]

KING: Yet the tough mind without the tender heart is incomplete. Lacking love, hard-hearted persons value people according to their usefulness. Self-centered, hard-hearted persons fail to experience the beauty of friendship.
IKEDA: You say that hardheartedness leads to depersonalization:

> The hardhearted individual never sees people as people, but rather as mere objects or as impersonal cogs in an ever-turning wheel. In the vast wheel of industry, he sees men as hands. In the massive wheel of big city life, he sees men as digits in a multitude. In the deadly wheel of army life, he sees men as numbers in a regiment. He depersonalizes life.[3]

KING: The ideal intellectual combines the toughness of the serpent with the tenderness of the dove. If we have only serpentlike qualities, we tend to be passionless, mean, and selfish. If we have only dovelike qualities, we tend be sentimental, anemic, and aimless. On the political level, the hardhearted are violent and bitter. Complacent do-nothings are soft-minded.
IKEDA: I see the synthesis of tough-mindedness and tender-heartedness as a Buddha-like state, a state of enlightenment. We both agree that the state of enlightenment is not a retreat into self, but a march into the lives of other people to better their predicaments.
KING: Without serpentlike qualities, we cannot solve the tough problems that riddle our world.
IKEDA: In the educational sphere, the best way to overcome fear of change is have people become comfortable with difference. That is why I see dialogue and cultural exchanges as bridges to understanding. I also endorse Dewey's idea of school activities bringing students in touch with real-life problems. Confronted with real-life problems, students cannot shrink into complacency so easily.

But from my perspective, dialogue and cultural exchanges work more effectively only when people have already undergone inner revolutions, which bring about an understanding of the connectedness of everything.
KING: People who realize that injustice anywhere is a threat to justice everywhere grasp the connectedness of all events.

IKEDA: In order to cooperate on a global level, people are going to have embrace changes as different cultures merge and form new cultural patterns. Soft-mindedness and hard-heartedness will have no place in this environment.

Twenty-Eight

PAULO FREIRE'S CIRCLES OF CERTAINTY

IKEDA: Martin Luther King, Jr. identifies fear of change as one of the glaring weaknesses of soft-mindedness. In your own thinking, you use the term "circles of certainty" to explain people who feel threatened if their truths are threatened and who suffer from an absence of doubt. Those caught in the web of "circles of certainty" you designate as "sectarians." Those who are not afraid to dialogue with others and want to transform reality you call "radicals."[1] Your pedagogy makes dialogue the centerpiece for all teaching and learning. The dynamism of dialogue re-creates knowledge and reality.

FREIRE: I want to rethink the whole relationship between teacher and student. The traditional model sees teachers as wholly active and students as wholly passive. Teachers place educational currency, information, into students as if they were banks. Students passively receive information, which is supposed to magically earn interest in their craniums.

IKEDA: What you have described simply creates soft-mindedness. Students don't confront, challenge, and evaluate what they have been taught. They fail to creatively address it. When students passively receive information yet do not make connections, then that account will not earn interest. The mind becomes rich only by creatively connecting different ideas.

When King talks about tough-mindedness, he refers to the keenly analytic mind that is open to new ideas. Your idea of radicalism has that notion within it, but strikes out in another, entirely different, direction. At the core of radicalization is the concept of *conscientização*, which means learning to perceive social, political, and economic contradictions and taking action against oppressive aspects of reality.[2]

A crucial part of radicalization consists of the search for contradictions. Your critics will contend that this search for contradictions turns people into fanatics or nihilists. Your counterclaim is that such a practice makes people critical.

FREIRE: Critical thinking throws people into their world, into real-world activities.

IKEDA: Like Dewey, you see education pursuits evolving around real-world issues.

FREIRE: That is true. But before we go there, we must begin elsewhere. Educational ventures can only begin in one place: with the reconciliation of the teacher-student relationship.

IKEDA: In *Pedagogy of the Oppressed*, you assert: "Education must begin with the solution of the teacher-student contradiction, reconciling the poles of the contradiction so that both are simultaneously teachers and students."[3]
FREIRE: This is the only atmosphere where true dialogue can flourish.
IKEDA: For you, dialogue is a discipline. It takes a good deal of self-mastery to engage in dialogue. The tendency in most people is to shut down when new ideas are introduced. The tendency in most people is to secretly afraid of anything that threatens their beliefs. The tendency is to crave inert ideas. Dialoguers embrace new ideas.
FREIRE: Dialoguers do more than embrace new ideas. They are the creators of new ideas.
IKEDA: Dialogue is based on love of the world and people, humility, faith in humankind and its ability to make and remake, hope, and critical thinking. I would call these superrational aspects of cognitive activity.
FREIRE: Without these facets, dialogue would not exist. Revolutionary educators must take pains to humanize all encounters in the classroom, to make them dialogical.
IKEDA: For you, educational activity is more than the development of critical thinking. Educational activity is the quest for mutual humanization. Overwhelming control in the classroom you even go so far as to say is necrophilic, as you state in *Pedagogy of the Oppressed*:

> Oppression—overwhelming control—is necrophilic; it is nourished by love of death, not life. The banking concept of education is also necrophilic. Based on a mechanistic, static, naturalistic, spatialized view of consciousness, it transforms students into receiving objects. It attempts to control thinking and action, leads women and men to adjust to the world, and inhibits their creative power.[4]

The banking concept of education is the basis for inert ideas. Love of death in some sense drives educators to discourage active thinking on the part of students. Love of life drives them to encourage active thinking in the form of dialogue. The love of life is the love of change and becoming change itself.
FREIRE: Inert ideas maintain the status quo. The status quo does not like active minds, dialogue, or re-creation of reality.
IKEDA: The state of Buddhahood exemplifies the love of life you describe. In the state of Buddhahood, compassion wells open from within and is the life force compelling us to enlighten others.
FREIRE: Such enlightenment would come through dialogue?
IKEDA: Yes. Thus the enlightened are dialoguers. Those who truly commiserate don't lock themselves up from the world. They go to others.
FREIRE: That is what dialogue is: going to others.
IKEDA: This is undoubtedly why you say:

The teacher's thinking is authenticated only by the authenticity of the students' thinking. The teacher cannot think for her students, nor can she impose her thought on them. Authentic thinking, thinking that is concerned about *reality*, does not take place in ivory towers in isolation, but only in communication.[5]

Twenty-Nine

HOWARD GARDNER'S MULTIPLE INTELLIGENCES

IKEDA: I am fascinated by your pluralistic account of intelligence. You reject the uniform view. The uniform view consists of a core curriculum, a set of facts everybody should know, and conventional means of assessment, including IQ tests. You attack three biases: Westist (putting reason and logic on a pedestal); Testist (valuing abilities only if they are testable); and Bestist (reduction of intelligence to one approach such as logical-mathematical thinking).[1]

GARDNER: Instead of reducing intelligence to the verbal and computational, I identify eight types of intelligence: linguistic intelligence (word smart); logical-mathematical intelligence (number/reasoning smart); spatial intelligence (picture smart); bodily-kinesthetic intelligence (body smart); musical intelligence (music smart); interpersonal intelligence (other smart); intrapersonal intelligence (self smart); and finally, naturalist intelligence (nature smart), which I have recently added.[2]

IKEDA: If your theory is correct . . .

GARDNER: If my theory is correct, then the classroom and educational milieus must be adjusted to include activities that match these intelligences. I see three new roles in the Multiple Intelligence (MI) educational environment: assessment specialist, student curriculum broker, and educational broker. The assessment specialist regularly evaluates students' abilities through a wide and diverse range of tests. Whereas the student-curriculum broker, upon reviewing the evaluation of the student curriculum broker, recommends what courses students should take, the educational broker discovers educational opportunities for students in the wider community. [3]

IKEDA: For example, music, cooperative learning, art activities, role-play, multimedia, field trips, and inner reflection.

GARDNER: Correct.

IKEDA: My general theory of education is not to teach the course, but to teach to students. If teachers operate according to verbal and computational model of intelligence alone, then so many people are going to be left out. That's unfathomable and unconscionable.

GARDNER: The traditional paradigm prevents us from seeing diversity of human intelligence.

IKEDA: It does more than that. I see it as an extremely oppressive model. If the traditional models of intelligence nourish only some of the people, in class, what about the others? They become intellectually starved and feel abandoned. The self-esteem of children who fall outside the golden group can only spiral downward.

GARDNER: My theory remedies that.

IKEDA: The core my educational philosophy, which reflects SGI's philosophy, is value creation. With your model of the intellect, more positive values can emerge in the classroom. This is because your model allows for all students to realize their potential. The quest for recognizing and realizing potential constitutes value-creating.

GARDNER: I believe that each of the intelligences is equally important.

IKEDA: I accept the idea that the unlocking of potentials is the kernel of education. As I said before, your pluralistic model brings more positive value in the world. I'm interested in the most desirable or highest intellectual states.

GARDNER: That would be placing the intellect into a hierarchy.

IKEDA: I realize that. But is there an ideal intellectual state toward which schooling should strive?

GARDNER: Once we recognize how the dynamic between the abilities of people and society's values and institutions impacts intelligence, then we will be more likely to support policies that help people achieve their potentials.[4]

IKEDA: Let me introduce a caveat to your optimism, not as stab at your theory but at the nature of institutions. Learning strategies fully reflecting your pluralism makes all intellectual capacities equal. This is at odds with verbal/computation model. Your model is inclusive; the other exclusive.

Your model not only creates a new paradigm for intellect, but a new paradigm for the intellectual. The intellectuals emerging from multiple intelligence schooling are at odds with the intellectual and intellectual hierarchy already in place and headed by a ruling class that makes huge profits off of computational expertise, for example. These new intellectuals, once they become prevalent, accepted, and promulgate in the mainstream, will reorient funding to accommodate the vast array of intellectual projects, not just those limited to the verbal and computational.

Moreover, the new intellectualism calls for a pluralistic balance and inclusion in the lowest and in the highest offices. If this is the case, then those in power won't be limited to those with verbal and computational skills. People of other intelligences will provide checks and balances.

GARDNER: I see where you're going.

IKEDA: People possessing interpersonal intelligences, for example, could change policies on war, health care, poverty, and many other issues. Those who are nature smart could undoubtedly change environmental issues. Policies wouldn't be dictated by the wordsmiths and the bean counters. More balanced policies could emerge.

GARDNER: My new paradigm would be amendable to globalism.

IKEDA: Quite amenable. Globalism depends upon people connecting. Your theory opens up tremendous possibilities for people to connect in different intellectual ways.
GARDNER: I would like to backtrack a little and maybe end with something you alluded to earlier—a higher intellectual state.
IKEDA: From my perspective, the highest intellectual state is Buddhahood. This is the consummation of intellect and compassion. This is the ideal toward which all people should strive. If the values of responsibility and humanity are enduring values, then the realization of these values is important in all kinds of intelligence. Intelligences are not developed value-free, but according to certain values. Responsibility and humanity undoubtedly suggest compassion. Compassionate wisdom is the zenith of self-mastery.
GARDNER: You have an agenda there.
IKEDA: Yes, admit I do. In the rhetoric of the development of human potential, we often neglect to realize why we desire to in the first place—because we believe human beings live more meaningful and richer lives when they reach their potential. Without compassion, people would try outrace each to achieve their potential first or at the expense of other people. The pluralistic cultivation of potentials can co-exist with the ethical cultivation of compassion.

Thirty

GEORGE DAVID MILLER'S REVOLUTIONARY BREAKS

IKEDA: I know that one of your principal concerns is how human beings bring about changes in their thinking. This obviously carries over into your educational philosophy.[1]

MILLER: It's an issue I take seriously. Learning is always a revolutionary activity because it means encountering and creating new ideas.

IKEDA: From your perspective, learning represents a cycle of breaks. Learning is at the same time a break from the familiar and secure and a stretching out toward the different or the alien.

MILLER: The security of the soft-minded consists of the sameness of familiar experience.

IKEDA: You describe, in other terms, Freire's "circles of certainty." In "circles of certainty," no doubt is allowed to enter. "Circles of certainty" are filled with inert ideas.

MILLER: When no doubts are allowed to enter the mind, no questions arise. How can people change without questioning themselves?

IKEDA: In the same way Dewey says children's minds are naturally active, you say that self-consciousness naturally flows from belief to doubt and from doubt to belief.

MILLER: I don't believe in close-mindedness. The mind is always partially open to new ideas: the cycle you just described, from belief to doubt and doubt to belief, can be narrowed but never shut. I believe in narrow minds, not closed minds.

IKEDA: You're saying that even the narrow-minded can change.

MILLER: Oh, sure, in nominal ways. The huge challenge we have is trying to prepare people to live of world of rapid change and frequent encounters with different cultures. In a global society, change is not an option—change is a necessity.

IKEDA: Being able to be comfortable with difference is a cardinal virtue for anyone educated in today's world.

MILLER: One of the things that you and I have to discuss is whether change comes about abruptly or a gradually.

IKEDA: I advocate a gradualist position.

MILLER: My question to you is whether you and I perhaps are saying the same thing. I don't believe human beings or civilization can transmogrify over night. Time is needed. The barbarian doesn't transform into a "cultured" person overnight.

IKEDA: I, too, believe in evolution.

MILLER: But the barbarian can evolve into even a more proficient killer or into a pacifist. The first evolution flows seamlessly; for the second evolution the end is not reached unless a dramatic change occurs. That change in different direction I call revolution.

IKEDA: While you are a gradualist when it comes to profound changes occurring over a long duration of time, you believe that directional changes occur rather abruptly.

MILLER: I'll use a mundane example to make my point. Perhaps I have lived a sedentary life and don't exercise at all. Then my doctor informs me I must exercise or my life will be shortened. I decide to change my ways because I realize my self-indulgences will hurt my family. On Tuesday I don't exercise at all. On Wednesday I begin with my exercise routine. The difference between Tuesday and Wednesday is a directional change in my life. Even if I take one baby step in another direction, it is still a step in another direction.

IKEDA: I like the metaphor of "baby steps." The first steps that babies take are radical because they have never taken them before. If we watch children when they take their first steps, they are clumsy and unbalanced. You also can see uncertainty in their eyes as each step is a new experience.

MILLER: When I think of changes, I like to think of the states of being. I ask myself: how do people evolve from one state of being to another? How does the person in hell change and evolve toward the higher states? From my perspective, this doesn't happen without altering directionality.

IKEDA: Which for you means an experience involving difference.

MILLER: Correct. I see the diasporic intellectual (which I believe all intellectuals in today's world must be) as someone trained in difference. In everyday educational activities, difference has to be modeled. Like you, I see inner revolution as the important first step. The most revolutionary thing we can do is to accept the transcending nature of our thinking into difference. In that way, we see that the dynamic nature of the human mind. Once we understand difference in ourselves as an intrinsic part of the human experience, we can accept it in other people and cultures.

IKEDA: One of the ways we can connect our philosophies is through the concept of self-control.

MILLER: Please explain.

IKEDA: You are describing a mastery of life of the mind. Difference, in all its forms, keeps the mind open. Sameness narrows the mind to slits. Self-mastery for you involves reaching out toward difference.

MILLER: The embracing for difference is the ultimate level of compassion. As I see it, the greatest compassion can embrace all differences. The embrace of compassion converts alien differences into familiar distinctions.

IKEDA: Compassion doesn't erase differences.

MILLER: Compassion revels in differences because those who are compassionate . . .

IKEDA: Already are aware of the differences in themselves. I can see what you're saying.

MILLER: You better explain it to me. I'm completely lost.

PART FOUR

MEETING TODAY'S EDUCATIONAL CHALLENGES ON IKEDA'S TERMS

Thirty-One

CHALK, ERASERS, AND VIOLENCE IN THE CLASSROOM

Violence knows no boundaries. Marquee violence—terrorism, rape, hate crimes, teen suicide, drive-by shootings, spousal and child abuse, and the incursion of bloodshed on school grounds—is no stranger even in wealthier nations. Violence against the self—as manifested in teen suicides and self-mutilation—is also prevalent. Even as wealth, possessions, and comforts accrue, violence still rears its ugly head. According to the New Zealand Foundation for Values Education Inc., New Zealand is a prime example of this phenomenon:

> Since 1960 our population has increased by 33 per cent; the gross domestic product has more than doubled; the government spending on education and wealth has risen dramatically. We are living longer, we are healthier than we have ever been, and we probably richer and more technologically sophisticated than most nations. But during the same period there has been a 400 per cent increase in violent crime; a 700% increase in births outside marriage; a tripling of children living in single-parent homes; the suicide rate of teenagers is four times higher; for one divorce in 1980 there are now six.[1]

The reasons for widespread violence are diverse. Some way the philosophy of radical individualism disconnects people from one another by promoting a survival of the fittest ethic. Ethical relativism, others say, allows anyone to justify any act. Extreme violence in movies and television programs encourages impressionable young people to act anti-socially—this is another popular line of argumentation. Along the same lines, music with references to Satan and demons, misogyny, and retaliation against police is sometimes blamed for violence. Other people will point to social class; others to economic deprivation; others to anomie and alienation. The predominance of an economic system cherishing things more than human beings is another. On a less theoretical level, social withdrawal, excessive feelings of rejection, and being a victim of violence contribute to violence.

Censorship, stiffer penalties, consistent standards of punishment, a return to the traditional nuclear family, teaching values, expanding love and violence, more adult supervision, a more equitable distribution of wealth, faculty, student, and parent coalitions—these are some of the standard remedies for violence in the classroom. One of the more interesting approaches to violence is the Sathya Sai Education in Human Values (SSEHV) in Scotland. The program calls for a "broadening of heart" as well as "expansion of love and universal compassion."[2]

Unique as the SSEHV, it continues to examine the issue of violence in terms of what external measures can be taken to make humans peaceful creatures. It fails to examine the issue from the reverse perspective: how self-control can promote nonviolence.

The idea of cultivating self-control is linked with the idea of cultivating wisdom. Personal enlightenment is linked to a greater sense of self and more intense feelings of compassion.

From Ikeda's perspective, the self is the place to begin the crusade against violence. While most other approaches work from the external world to the internal or psychological world, Ikeda's approach starts from the internal world and pushes out into the external world. The evolution of self from the four evil paths to the more compassionate stages of (human beings, heavenly beings, voice-hearers, cause-awakened ones, and bodhisattvas) form the basis for peaceful interaction with others.

The road toward the higher states consists of a keen understanding of karma. Our thoughts, words, and deeds don't occur in a vacuum, but in a web of interconnections that eventually come back and reverberate in our lives. Even if some education rejects the afterlife aspect of karma, it can still incorporate karma with respect to personal, environmental, economic, and political issues.

Didacticism or moralizing is not the suggested means for eliminating violence. Being told what to do fails to cultivate judgment, being able to assess the consequences, short and long-term. Understanding karma offers a greater perspective as to the consequences of our violent acts. We must exercise self-control so that violent karmic forces don't turn back on us.

Moralizing cannot bring people to understand the nature of compassion. Teaching people to be absolutists and that life has unconditional value is not the same as creating and broadening the heart. Broadening the heart is an individual journey that can be guided by external sources but is ultimately navigated by individuals.

Mastery of self, consisting of karmic comprehension and the evolution beyond the four evil states, provides a positive beginning to the problem of violence. External controls suggest that human beings are unable to control themselves. It sends a negative message. Mastery of self emphasizes that individuals can make positive changes from their own energy.

According to this perspective, mastery of self is the trellis and external controls grow up and around the guiding force. Mastery of self is identical to compassionate wisdom.

Thirty-Two

SELF-ESTEEM AND THE ENDURING SELF

Education systems interested in the dignity of students and human development closely monitor levels of self-esteem. Schooling designed to create little geniuses, who accomplish Herculean tasks but despise themselves, fails to cultivate the full spectrum of human personality. The purpose of value-creating education is to develop an enduring sense of self. The quest for an enduring sense of self can be called the search for self-esteem. Yet this concept of self-esteem offers a new concept of self.

Low self-esteem arises from many diverse sources. People buried under criticism are often bearers of self-esteem. Those who fail to receive affection, support, respect, and encouragement fall prone to low self-esteem. Those who are bullied by others—ridiculed, picked on, and teased—are susceptible. Other susceptible groups include: targets of verbal, physical, sexual, or emotional abuse; recipients of age-inappropriate punishments; those who are shamed, ignored, threatened with abandonment, have their feelings ignored, or are unable to participate in "regular" activities because of illness.

According to The Self-Esteem Institute, low self-esteem can be a strong factor in the development of an unstable emotional life characterized by fear, anxiety, anger, panic attacks, and depression. As has been widely reported, low self-esteem is tied to eating disorders like anorexia and bulimia. Low self-esteem can play a role in child-abuse, domestic violence, and teen and gang violence.[1]

One of the major criticisms of self-esteem programs is that they emptily and gratuitously affirm students. Affirming people apart from their accomplishments lowers academic standards as students become more interested in doing what makes them feel good instead of striving for excellence. The product of such programs is often student complacency.

Feel-good self-esteem programs only help people to accept themselves, which is far different from affirming the self. When we accept ourselves, we can passively endure everything that we have done in our lives. We accept what we have done and what those events have made us: we accept our history. For example, we may have done many things that have hurt other people or ourselves—and we must endure what we have done.

Acceptance of self is more like looking into the window of lives and watching it like we watch television—in a passive, uncreative way. Affirmation of self is like becoming a creator of television shows and is oriented toward the future because it involves changing oneself.

Self-esteem as self-affirmation can also be understood as revolution of self, to borrow Ikeda's concept. Building self-esteem means building a revolutionary force within ourselves that constantly renew and invigorates the context of our lives. The force within is more than assertive; it is creative and encompasses all aspects of our lives

The object of self-esteem will determine whether the self-esteem can withstand the vicissitudes of existence. If the sense of self is tied into things that can easily be taken away from us, then self-esteem is at peril. Athletes who determine their worth only according to their athletic accomplishments can easily have their self-esteem stripped from them. The same can be said of actors and politicians who value themselves according to the awards they receive or the elections they win.

Founded on a shallow and shaky foundation, self-esteem flounders. For self-esteem to be lasting, it must be founded on the greater self. The greater self is connected with all life and all beings. The self-esteem of the greater self exhibits a self integrated with the flow of the universe.

The greater the self-esteem, the greater the sense of the greater self. Bearers of low self-esteem are on the defensive so much and so desperately trying to affirm themselves that their principal concern is themselves. On a hierarchy of self-esteem, they reside on the lower levels. They cannot withstand change and desire sameness.

Just as those at the bottom of Maslow's hierarchy of needs can only fulfill physical needs, so people at the bottom of a self-esteem hierarchy can barely subsist on their low levels of self-esteem. In the same way people at the top of Maslow's hierarchy can reach for their full potential, so people at the top of the self-esteem hierarchy can reach the full sense of self.

People with high self-esteem (founded on the greater self) are compassionate. The reason they are compassionate is because their self of sense is so strong that they can give to others without feeling that this giving somehow shrinks the self. Compassion actually expands our state of being. Compassion is not to be confused with trying to live in the lives of others because our lives are painful or we don't want to face ourselves.

From Ikeda's perspective, the cultivation of self-esteem is the cultivation of the greater self. This is not the gratuitous celebration of self or the glorification of rugged individualism, but the emergence of the cosmic self.

In this era of globalism, self-esteem has to be understood in a broader context. In the larger sense, self-esteem allows people to enter into dialogue with difference and not be diminished by it. Difference diminishes people with low self-esteem because they need to defend themselves from attacks to the slender isle of self.

Difference enhances people with high self-esteem: difference can be transformed into an even greater enhancement of self. For those with low esteem, people with different values and beliefs as diminish their self-worth. value.

For people with high self-esteem, different values and beliefs enhance their self-worth.

Thirty-Three

REDUCTIONISM AND COMPARTMENTALIZATION

Tribalism, provincialism, ethnocentrism, and isolationism—these may be the four evil paths for twentieth-first century education. The ideal citizens of the twenty-first century are not NIMBY (NOT IN MY BACKYARD) citizens, who only care if something directly affects them. The new citizenry, cosmopolitan citizens, adopt an EMBY (EVERYTHING'S MY BACKYARD) worldview.

EMBY education transcends national boundaries and seeks values applicable to all humanity. Beliefs in the superiority of one's own country, contempt for difference, the imposition of values on "ignorant" peoples, and the desire to withdraw and not cooperate work at cross-purposes with the EMBY worldview. For Ikeda, the EMBY worldview includes the major military, economic, and environmental issues facing humanity:

> Education for peace should reveal the cruelty of war, emphasize the threat of nuclear weapons and insist on the importance of arms reduction. Education for development must deal with the eradication of hunger and poverty and should devote attention to establishing a system of economic welfare for approximately five hundred million people who suffer from malnutrition today and two-thirds of all nations that are impoverished. Harmony between humanity and nature should be the theme of education in relation to the environment. It is important to bring the most serious consideration to the extent to which nuclear explosions harm the ecosystem. Learning to respect the dignity of the individual must be the cornerstone of education in relations to human rights.[1]

One of the ways to bring about an EMBY worldview is through cross-cultural courses and experiences, such as Study Abroad. Another is through interdisciplinary courses, which compel students to find and draw connections. Both of these approaches are being applied in the curriculum of Soka University of America, as they are at many institutions.

The fundamental question of twenty-first century educators is: How can the experience of difference be transformed into the experience of commonality? Cross-cultural and interdisciplinary courses and face-to-face encounters with different people compel students to re-examine their own beliefs.

Compartmentalization amputates a part from the whole and vivisects that part. Reductionism oversimplifies and refuses to acknowledge the baroque intersections of issues. The vivisection of intellectual issues leads to sterility and banality. The reduction of intellectual issues into oversimplified final answers offers solutions that fail to cover the breadth or descend to the depth of matters. When compartmentalization and reductionism become embedded in political and social thought, then the outcome is tribalism, provincialism, ethnocentrism, and isolationism—and a NIMBY philosophy.

Reductionism and compartmentalization are symptoms of a closed heart, as Ikeda says:

> A person with a closed heart is one who is shut up within a self-imposed shell of selfishness and complacency. This sad and pointless act of severing self and other bears the hallmark of evil. . . . This deep-rooted tendency . . . is manifested in a singular way in our time.[2]

When manifested on a larger social level, the closed heart plays out in nationalism and ethnic identity ploys.

Internal revolution can play a central role in fostering holism. Inner revolution always assumes individuals as a process moving toward higher states of being. In self-revolt, we break away from one pattern of behavior and worldview and embrace another. Our familiarity with change and difference in our own lives allows us to be open to others.

The internal revolution can be fostered by educational practices. Instead of holding final exams in isolated classrooms in which people have no idea what the other is doing, a temporary museum could be set up such that all students in the university (or institutions in the area) could present their projects to each other. The final exam would include drawing connections between diverse projects. Students would be able to see the diversity of their universities and the interconnections between the parts. Dialogue would naturally flow from such an environment and holism need not be forced.

Academic holism is sterile and mechanical. It compiles perspectives, and only vaguely and shallowly integrates them. Spiritual holism emerges from compassion. It seeks out other perspectives and differences wanting interaction not simply for the accumulation of knowledge or wisdom, but for improvement of others. Spiritual holism is not an academic exercise, but an ethical enterprise.

The transformation from academic to spiritual holism is marked by the transformation from a NIMBY philosophy to an EMBY perspective. Spiritual holism says more than everything is interconnected; it says that each of us is interconnectivity.

Thirty-Four

NIHILISM AND APATHY

At the end of nineteenth century, Nietzsche forecasted another 200 years of nihilism. Unlike many weather forecasts and without the aid of Doppler radar, Nietzsche's forecast has held true at least for the first 100 or so years.

When the highest values no longer have any value, then nihilism is the result. Values once residing at the top of value hierarchies—belief in a supreme being and the afterlife, the dignity of life, moral progress, beloved community, and freedom for all human beings—take terrible tumbles and are rendered virtually worthless. The devaluation of these leading values is similar to the devaluation of stocks when the market spirals into a depression. When the highest values tumble into spiritual depression, then the economy of the spiritual life falters. The economy of the spiritual life is driven by its leading values.

To borrow a metaphor from a preceding chapter but to contort it for another use, leading values are the trellis on which other values grow and intertwine. The structure leading values provide for all values confers meaning on the value experience. The meaning of life is tied up in the structure of values. A meaningless life corresponds to meaningless a value structure. The meaningful life corresponds to a meaningful value structure.

From a Makiguchian perspective, the more positive values we bring into the world, the positive, the more meaningful, our lives will be. The production of ancillary values (pleasure and utility values) cannot bring about meaning: only the leading values can. The leading values are the spiritual values, referring to the ideals and not the stomachs of human beings.

But why care when "nothing matters anyway?" The "nothing matters anyway" belief becomes the leading idea and value of nihilism. In this new de-spiritualized economy, only brown dead things cling to the trellis of nihilism. The new de-spiritualized economy produces one product much more than any other—apathy. Who cares? Why try? What does it really matter?

One of the standard responses to nihilism is to return to traditional values and beliefs. That strategy can be questioned on three major counts. In the first place, beliefs that don't resonate in people, fail to strike the core of their being because they don't emerge from life experiences, are inert ideas, as Whitehead says. Inert ideas aren't going to move anyone. Secondly, the return to the past is often accompanied by sectarianism, ethnocentrism, and isolationism. These attitudes, which tend to produce "circles of certainty," are at odds with globalism and cosmopolitan citizenship. Globalism and cosmopolitan citizenship are future-oriented, seeing dialogue and cooperation as means for creating a vibrant, interconnected global civilization.

If education is meant to cultivate people who care and want to make a difference in the world, then it must treat nihilism.

Wisdom-based education is the fundamental means to treat spiritual malaise. Ultimate values issues take priority in wisdom-based education.

In the current scheme of things, wisdom-based education cannot function. In many realms, intelligence has not been extended to include wisdom. Yet leading values have wisdom as their core. Wisdom is the minister of the spiritual economy. It integrates values so that they wind themselves around a trellis of meaning.

Politically Correct (PC) classrooms are a hindrance to wisdom-based education. PC purges dialogue of its spontaneity, as people sit on pins and needles wondering whether what they're going to say is going to offend anybody. They learn to censor any idea that may in some roundabout way can be interpreted to offend somebody. Wisdom-based education demands that dialogue be heard on all issues and include unpopular or extreme positions. Wisdom-based education places trust in dialogue as the means for creating community and confronting, tolerating, and even embracing differences.

One of the leading values of wisdom-based education could stem from what Ikeda calls "an ethos of symbiosis":

> In East Asian culture, a way of looking at the world inherited from Confucianism that is shared throughout the region might be called an "ethos of symbiosis." I am talking about the kind of mentality that favors harmony over opposition, unity over division, "we" over "I." Practically, it is expressed as the idea that human beings should live in harmony with one another and with nature. With such mutual support, the entire community flourishes.[1]

An ethos of symbiosis can counteract values of extreme individualism, narcissism, and consumerism that have greatly indulged the lesser self, but have barely reached the greater self. From a worldview stressing connectivity, harmony, and commonality, leading values can more easily emerge because such a worldview strikes a chord of hope within in each of us. Once the chord of hope is struck, we can see the potential of things and often the ultimate potential of things.

Wisdom-based education can create a philosophy of hope that counteracts the despair of nihilism. These are not the smaller hopes of the lesser self, but the greater hopes of the greater self, which recognizes that the greatest hope in humanity lies within each of us:

> The human spirit is endowed with the ability to transform even the most difficult circumstances, creating value and ever richer meaning. When each person brings this limitless spiritual capacity to full flower, and

when ordinary citizens unite in a commitment to positive change, a century of peace—a century of life—will come into being.[2]

Thirty-Five

INTOLERANCE

In "The Arrogance of the Present," Ikeda observes that human wisdom has been confined to the areas of science and technology, but rarely extended to self-understanding. While the Hubble telescope can observe activity in distant galaxies, we often fail to understand our basic human nature. We are most distant from ourselves, Nietzsche asserts. In the same vein, Ikeda contends that

> in areas where human wisdom is most needed, it seems to be least in evidence, and so suffering and discontent are prolonged or even intensified. What is the reason for this channeling of human wisdom into certain areas alone? Doesn't it seem peculiar that we can solve the problems of the universe and the heavenly bodies and yet are unable to solve the mystery of a single human being?[1]

The incalculable number of wars, indifference to our fellow beings, and self-destruction (as neuroses and psychoses consume us) demonstrate how little we understand ourselves.

In the lower states of being, tolerance is all that low-level life forces can muster. With low levels of compassion, the best we can do from an ethical standpoint is to endure others. Tolerance represents the beginning of self-mastery: enduring difference and respecting the rights, opinions, and practices of others. Just as a cartwheel is tremendous feat for the beginner in gymnastics, so tolerance is a tremendous feat for the beginner in ethics. While it takes self-mastery to do a cartwheel and practice tolerance, it takes even a greater degree of self-mastery to do back flips and to be compassionate.

Permitting an action is different from understanding an action. "Permitting" can suggest contempt, nose turned up as if smelling a bad odor. Permitting suggests accepting, but placing at arm's length. This can be likened to the difference between acceptance and affirmation of ourselves. We accept what we cannot change; we endure it. The act of affirmation is a remaking of self, a creative act. Acceptance of self is a spectator sport; affirmation of self is the sport of remaking self.

"Enduring" is an outside-in activity, contrary to the inside-out activity characteristic to inner human revolution. Inner human revolution is each person's remaking of herself and thus remaking the world. The remaking comes from deep levels of compassion immersing us in the underlying life force.

Tolerance represents the first stage of human ethical development. Tolerance steps beyond egoism, ethnocentrism, and nationalism. It respects the rights, opinions, and practices of others. If the ideal for humanity is an abstract and distant understanding, tolerance is the virtue of choice.

If the ideal is kinship with others, not merely understanding them as we understand distant galaxies through telescopes, then something more than tolerance is needed. Ikeda calls this "respectful compassion." The difference between tolerance and respectful compassion is similar to the difference Martin Luther King, Jr. draws between desegregation and integration:

> However, when the *desegregation* process is one hundred percent complete, the human relations dilemma of our nation will still be monumental unless we launch now the parallel thrust of the of the integration process. . . .
>
> *Desegregation* is eliminative and negative, for it simply removes these legal and social prohibitions. Integration is creative, and is therefore more profound and far-reaching than desegregation. Integration is the positive acceptance of desegregation and the welcomed participation of Negroes into the total range of human activities. Integration is genuine intergroup, interpersonal doing.[2]

Tolerance is not the virtue for "genuine, intergroup, interpersonal doing." Tolerance is not engagement with others. The words "eliminative" and "negative" fit tolerance well. In some ways, "tolerance" suggests a "hands off" approach—non-interference.

Tolerance is a step up from the narrow-mindedness of intolerance that prevents dialogue, the essence of our humanity: Being close-mindedness robs people of the ability to dialogue with others—a capacity that can be considered proof of our humanity.

Self-mastery is a prerequisite for true dialogue:

> True dialogue is only possible when both parties are committed to self-mastery. But there is another essential element without which dialogue becomes manipulative rhetoric: no matter how culturally different they are from oneself or seemingly opposed to one's own interest.[3]

Lower degrees of self-mastery involve allowing people with different opinions to express themselves. Difference strikes hard at the lesser selves. For lesser selves, it remains a challenge to endure difference. Higher degrees of self-mastery allow for more than enduring difference without squelching it. The greater self that compassionately connects with the universe embraces difference.

True dialogue involves "genuine intergroup, interpersonal doing." Tolerance, as an impersonal virtue, is inappropriate for true dialogue. In his 2000 Peace Proposal, *Peace through Dialogue, A Time to Talk*, Ikeda recognizes that the antidote for deep-seated global conflicts is not tolerance but proactive and dynamic efforts to achieve peace:

> Any attempt to unravel differences and confrontations as complex as these must be grounded in something far more solid than passive acceptance or tolerance. Such attitudes cannot possibly provide the basis for a culture of peace or a new global civilization that will enrich the lives of people far into the third millennium.[4]
>
> Peace cannot be a mere stillness, a quiet interlude between wars. It must be a vital and energetic arena of life-activity, won through our own volitional, proactive efforts.[5]

CONCLUSION

Theory, no matter how rich, has to have practical application for educators. When educators leave conferences scratching their heads and wondering just how in the world those great ideas they have been listening to for hours are going to help them in their school systems, their schools, and their classrooms, then something is amiss. This is why I wanted to conclude this book with a number of possible creative applications of Daisaku Ikeda's philosophy of education. The purpose of this chapter is to develop possible practical implications of Ikeda's educational theory for administrators, teachers, and students.

1. International Education

Enlightened educators from all over the world should form an international society dedicated to the major aspects of Ikeda's philosophy of education:

(1) All beings can be enlightened.
(2) The ultimate goal of education is to help students create happiness.
(3) Happiness is realized by creating values.
(4) Value creation is fueled by inner revolution.
(5) Inner revolution is the Socratic quest to know thyself and to use dialogue as tool to achieve that objective (which is wisdom)
(6) Inner revolution is the result of self-mastery.
(7) Cosmic kinship and citizenship are by-products of inner revolution and represent the core of peace.
(8) Karmic understanding especially as it relates to thinking is requisite for the cessation of spiritual violence.
(9) The ten states of being serve as indicator of the spiritual growth of a person.
(10) Peaceful competition is the means for spiritual growth and cosmic citizenship.

The educational equivalent of the United Nations should be created to implement major aspects of Ikeda's philosophy of education. Starting as and remaining a grass roots organization, this cadre of diverse educators from the four corners of the world and representing primary, secondary, and post-secondary education will begin the task of developing a cosmic pedagogy.

2. School Systems

Many school systems are plagued by violence. The means to end physical violence is to put an end to spiritual violence. "If only we knew that so-and-so was prone to violence, we would have helped him. We didn't know" is the tale of woe related by the survivors while standing in pools of blood. The physical violence will abate when the spiritual violence declines.

A vigorous campaign against nihilism, cynicism, apathy, despair, mistrust, and indifference must be waged. These forms of spiritual decay can be termed spiritual terrorism. This campaign cannot work without a keen understanding of the spiritual development of each person. The ten states of being, with a little tweaking, provide an instrument for evaluating Spiritual IQ. More than pigeonholing people in this state of being or that one or that is the attempt to gauge their temporal-spatial experience.

In the lower states of being, people experience the slowness of time and space as constricted. In the higher states of being, people experience the rapidity of time and space as expansive. In the lower states of being, people are narcissistic and disconnected. In the higher states of being people transcend the shell of their egos and feel more and more connected with the world. The more connectivity, the more spirituality. The more spiritual, the compassionate and the less prone to violent.

In what follows, a sample of the Spiritual IQ Test will be attempted.

Does time go quickly for you or seem to drag on forever?
(general question to gauge spatial breadth)
When does time go quickly for you?
(general question to gauge flow to temporal experience)
When does it seem to drag on?
Are the only times you feel "bigger" are you're angry?
(sign of *asura* or warlike demons)
Are many of your actions based instincts?
(sign of the state of animals)
Do you care about the next generation?
Do you feel invincible?
(sign of heavenly beings)
Do you feel helpless most of the time?
(sign of hell)
Do you feel so connected to others such that their pain usually affects you, even people you don't know, who live in other parts of the world?
(sign of the bodhisattva state)

Spiritual IQ needs to be assessed on a regular basis. With rigorous empirical evidence, it may one day be proven that people whose answers consistently land them on the four evil paths suggests they are potentially violent human beings.

In addition to Spiritual IQ, Karmic IQ must also be assessed. Every action is meaningful. Not one thing we think, say, or do is insignificant. It not only impacts our behavior but the behavior of others. Being able to assess the consequences of our actions and words are the most obvious indicators of Karmic IQ. But the subtlety of Karmic IQ concerns the consequences of thinking and how it affects us. The inner spiritual world is the basis for our words and deeds. Words and deeds for the person primarily in the state of hell, for example, will reflect the fundamental criteria of the state.

3. The General Curriculum

All general curricula should aim at wisdom as the ultimate objective. Wisdom should not be conceived as a far-away capstone experience to be completed after the "real" learning (information and knowledge) and "real" courses occur. Nor should it be ghettoized in philosophy or religion departments. Nor should there be an allotted time for "wisdom" to emerge during a specific time during class, as if after the important work is done a little extra time is to be allotted for "wisdom."

The most important element of a wisdom-based education is a question-friendly educational environment in which the process of learning (dialogue, question-posing, and conflict) is as important as the product of learning (exams, papers, projects). The key point is to develop a flexible and fluid learning continuum dramatizing the interconnectedness of human learning endeavors—information, knowledge, and wisdom. Such holism will be difficult to execute with a limited Spiritual IQ.

Those who have difficulty seeing that the universe is interconnected will find it difficult to see the interconnectedness of all areas of learning. A wisdom-based curriculum is less about curricula mechanically interconnected in well planned and executed syllabi, but is more about educators with a vision of the whole that they bring to the educational enterprise. Holistic thinkers create holistic curricula. Their spiritual vision of whole automatically propels them to this project.

4. Teachers and Students

The ten principles should play a prominent role in all interactions with students and selection of materials. Whatever choices are made, for example, they must produce value in the classroom. The highest values represent the higher rungs of the ten states of being. In order to reach those levels, students must be encouraged to enact inner revolutions. They must understand the relationship between their karmic predicament and the ten states of being by a combination of self-exploration and dialogue. Petty inducements (grades, honors for good grades, and the material possessions for which good grades are bartered) fail to motivate the students to enact inner revolution and discover wisdom. This can be accomplished by introducing a belief and value system emphasizing self-assessment. Students must be encouraged to build self-esteem in the sense of developing the greater self.

5. Addendum

Daisaku Ikeda's philosophy of education provides the building blocks for the spiritualization of education. All this means is that we will once again search for the true meaning of life, which is contained in the inward journey toward wisdom and Buddhahood.

EPILOGUE

Mark Roelof Eleveld

George David Miller is an innovator of thought. He does things his own way. Writing about higher education in America as well as globally, he is unafraid of instituting critique, and does not play patsy to the passivity of recognized academy scholars. Despite such indignation for the current system, his credentials are irreproachable. He is the author of two excellent books on education, a global handbook on ethics as well as an idiosyncratic inquiry on ethical thought, and is a published poet. No doubt, a writer of this sort has a novel or two laying in waiting. Although the desire amongst petty colleagues will be to ignore him, to point at him as if he were entering a cave with "his eyes full of darkness" looking "ridiculous," it will be difficult to discount this well-learned gadfly who so keenly observes higher education.

But Miller is neither a cynic nor anarchist, and his passion toward a worldview carries him well beyond the limitations of academia. He is not carrying on for the sake of the self-professed, academic insiders who never tire of self-congratulations—although they will find themselves listening, as this book rains much heavy fire. Instead, Miller places himself in a bigger thinking, hopeful community, calling to the ideals of Jesus of Nazareth, Mohandas Karamchand Gandhi, Tsunesaburo Makiguchi, Josei Toda, Martin Luther King, Jr., Daisaku Ikeda, those of both the ideological and politically motivated alike. Revolutionary human being help others achieve enlightenment, not because of a sterile moral imperative to help others. "Full enlightenment," Miller writes, "consists of fully—intellectually and spiritually—recognizing our bond with all beings in the universe. We identify the self with the universe. Consequently, the higher levels of wisdom expand self from our physical needs to the needs of other beings, whether sentient or nonsentient" (p. 53).

Older, distinguished teachers may be critical of this sort of idealistic style—moral imperative, revolutionary, spiritually—but behind such scoffing toward this language hides our own dwelling in the inner recesses of misery. When academics fail, they blind themselves in the impoverished world of the underground, feeling themselves only through the lowering and subjugation of others: "The more conscious I was of goodness, and of all that sublime and beautiful, the more deeply I sank into my mire and the more capable I became of sinking into it completely," screams the failed searcher of truth. Distinguishing between "oughts" and "is," Miller is strongest in his offerings for enlightenment, joining Ikeda in believing it is possible, now. He distances himself when he merges philosophical enterprises, and flexes his mental might when fusing

Eastern and Western. In Miller, you find not a dismissal of Western principle as much as a synthesis between two, as offered through his historical readings of Tsunesaburo Makiguchi, Nichiren Daishonin, and, most recently, Daisaku Ikeda. Beneath each lies the Socratic project with a Nietzschian cutting.

Miller steps up to the task during his creation and interpretation of the ten states of being, opening doors to self-evaluation and salvation. Within this paradigm we find mirrors, frightening and distinguishing of whom we are and, perhaps more importantly, who we can be. And his handling of nihilism and apathy, butted up against the current educational system make sense. In fact, his revelations are scathing:

> Moralizing cannot bring people to understand the nature of compassion. Teaching people to be absolutists and that life has unconditional value is not the same as creating and broadening the heart. Broadening the heart is an individual journey that can be guided by external sources but is ultimately navigated by individuals. (p. 134)

As a scholar he intends to enlighten us but as a writer he has learned from the Greeks the value of entertainment. Miller is most alive during the dialogues between Ikeda and other thinkers of a global world. But this book is not written as much by a scholar, cold and sterile in his attempts. No, this writing is the creation of a writer willing to take chances at every corner. It is a risky book of ideas, speaking for others in his voice, but it reminds us that the sources of the truest truths must always be confirmed on a personal level. Academics, prizewinners and radicals alike, seldom offer themselves up for such scrutiny. Within these pages, Miller has shown himself interacting with these ideas publicly and frankly as an individual, as a human being. He drops himself down from no clouds. He is ingrained in the soot of human creativity and human error as well as enlightenment. So Miller is a grunt in the battlefield of our educational times, and as such, very open for me to read. As some have said, he walks the walk.

It is the enterprise of philosophical thinking to alter viewpoints. To hold ideals and values accountable for the decisions and world that operates around us. But students hold these truths beyond them, finding the close account of truth too revealing for their own taste. "How can such ideas help me? What does this do for me at work? How does it help me make more money? How can it help me acquire a bigger house? Why should I question everything in life, in order to find a true path? Ikeda talks about human revolution that each individual should face in his search. I believe that I try to open that door by having them question. Through questioning comes dialogue and through dialogue comes a deeper understanding of themselves and the other students in the class. In his concluding pages, Miller affirms such value inquiry and tries to answer for the educator and layman alike:

> Theory, no matter how rich, has to have practical applications for educators. When educators leave conferences scratching their heads and wondering just how in the world those great ideas they have been listening to for hours are going to help them in their school systems, their schools, and their classrooms, then something is amiss. . . .
>
> All general curricula should aim at wisdom as the ultimate objective. Wisdom should not be received as a far-away capstone experience to be completed after the "real" learning (information and knowledge) and "real" courses occur. Nor should it be ghettoized in philosophy or religion departments. Nor should there be an allotted time for "wisdom" to emerge during a specific time during class, as if after the important work is done a little extra time is to allotted for "wisdom. . . ."
>
> Whatever choices are made, for example, they must produce value in the classroom. . . .
>
> Petty inducements (grades, honors for good grades, and the material possession for which good grades are bartered) fail to motivate the students to enact inner revolution and discover wisdom. (pp. 151, 153, 154)

This book makes an important statement and will be studied critically by supporters and nay Sayers alike. Whether or not the conclusions are agreed upon by the majority, this writing provides a direction toward discussion, not a superficial surfacing of the Japanese traditions of Ikeda's philosophy or the inertia of an apathetic world education, but a richly articulated, historically trustful summary of Soka Gakkai's philosophical buildings and Daisaku Ikeda's higher mental life in the global world.

After all, it is through George David Miller's writings that the Western world will come to know Daisaku Ikeda's philosophy of education. An early introduction came by way of the Peace Exhibit orchestrated by Lawrence Edward Carter, Sr. This truly impressive exhibit, albeit slightly intimidating, features the peace pursuits of Mohandas Gandhi, Martin Luther King, Jr., and Daisaku Ikeda. In this superstar lineup of profoundly influential pacifists, Ikeda is new to the forefront of American minds, putting him on stage and his philosophical ideas and educational philosophy under scrutiny.

Why Daisaku Ikeda? What does he bring to the table of educational thought? This is an enormous charge for Miller to answer. The first

Western written comprehensive text of Ikeda's philosophy, Miller's task is grave: How the Western world comes to know and understand Ikeda will be largely based upon how this text is received and interpreted.

Then, to the task that Miller puts before us as the reader: What does Buddhism offer as a beginning to Ikeda's humanism and how does it transform into individual and societal enlightenment toward spiritual humanism?

NOTES

Foreword

1. Martin Luther King, Jr. *Where Do We Go From Here: Chaos or Community* (New York: Harper & Row, 1967), p. 167.

2. W.E.B. DuBois, *The Souls of Black Folk* in *Three Negro Classics* (New York: Avon Books, 1965), p. 268.

Introduction

1. Daisaku Ikeda, *Soka Education: A Buddhist Vision for Teachers, Students and Parents* (Santa Monica, Cal.: Middleway Press, 2001), p. 90.

2. *Ibid.*, p. 130.

3. *Ibid.*, p. 180.

4. *Ibid.*, p. 184.

5. *Ibid.*

6. *Ibid.*, p. 179.

Chapter One

1. Philip B. Yampolsky, Introduction to *Selected Writings of Nichiren*, ed. Philip B. Yampolsky (New York: Columbia University Press, 1990), pp. 1-10.

2. Burton Watson, Introduction to *Letters of Nichiren*, trans. Burton Watson and others (New York: Columbia University Press, 1996), pp. 1-18.

3. Introduction to *The Writings of Nichiren Daishonin*, editor-translator The Gosho Translation Committee (Tokyo: Soka Gakkai, 1999), pp. xvii-xxxi.

4. Nichiren Daishonin, *Letters of Nichiren*, trans. Burton Watson and others (New York: Columbia University Press, 1996), p. 480.

5. Nichiren Daishonin, *The Writings of Nichiren Daishonin*, editor-translator The Gosho Translation Committee (Tokyo: Soka Gakkai, 1999), p. 3.

6. Daisaku Ikeda, as quoted in N. Radhakrishnan, *Daisaku Ikeda, The Man and His Mission* (Delhi: National Center for Development Education, 1992), p. 108.

7. René Huyghe and Daisaku Ikeda, *Dawn After Dark*, trans. Richard L. Gage (New York: Weatherhill, 1991), p. 210.

8. Johan Galtung and Daisaku Ikeda, *Choose Peace: A Dialogue Between Johan Galtung and Daisaku Ikeda* (London and East Haven, Conn., 1995), p. 63.

9. Daisaku Ikeda, *A Lasting Peace*, Vol. 2 (New York and Tokyo: Weatherhill, 1987), p. 83.

10. Daishonin, *The Writings*, p. 4.

11. Daisaku Ikeda, Foreword to *The Writings of Nichiren Daishonin*, p. xii.

12. Daishonin, *The Writings*, p. 280.

Chapter Two

1. Dayle M. Bethel. *Makiguchi: The Value Creator* (New York and Tokyo: Weatherhill, 1973, 1994), p. 40.

2. *Ibid.*, pp. 28-29.

3. *Ibid.*, p. 98.

4. *Ibid.*, pp. 32-37; 44-45.

5. *Ibid.*, p. 93.

6. Frederick Edwords, "What Is Humanism?" http://humanist.net/definitions. humanism. html

7. *Humanist Manifesto I.* http://humanist.net/documents/manifesto.1.html

8. "Definitions of Humanism." http://secularspirituality.org/spirituality/humanism.html.

9. Dayle M. Bethel, Introduction to Tsunesaburo Makiguchi, *Education for Creative Living: Ideas and Proposals for Tsunesaburo Makiguchi*, trans. Alfred Birnbaum, ed. Dayle M. Bethel (Ames, Iowa: Iowa University Press, 1989), pp. 4-12.

10. *Humanist Manifesto I.*

11. *Ibid.*

12. Makiguchi, *Education for Creative Living*, p. 17.

13. *Ibid.*, p. 19.

14. *Humanist Manifesto I.*

15. *Ibid.*

16. Makiguchi, *Education for Creative Living*, p. 29.

17. *Ibid.*, p. 42.

18. Bethel, *Makiguchi*, pp. 49-50.

19. Makiguchi, *Education for Creative Living*, pp. 19-20.

20. *Ibid.*, p. 20.

21. *Ibid.*, p. 106.

22. *Ibid.*, p. 168.

23. *Humanist Manifesto I.*

24. Makiguchi, *Education for Creative Living*, pp. 19-20.

25. *Ibid.*, pp. 97-98.

Chapter Three

1. Daisaku Ikeda and Arnold Toynbee, *Choose Life: A Dialogue*, ed. Richard L. Gage (Oxford: Oxford University Press, 1976), p. 91.

2. *Ibid.*, p. 89.

3. *Ibid.*, p. 91.

Chapter Four

1. Daisaku Ikeda, *Life: An Enigma, a Precious Jewel*, trans. Charles S. Terry (Tokyo, New York, London: Kodansha, 1982), pp. 41, 91, 147, 163, 219, 226.

2. Daisaku Ikeda, *Unlocking the Mysteries of Birth and Death: Buddhism in the Contemporary World* (London: Warner Books, 1988), pp. 113-114; 117-128; 178-180.

Chapter Five

1. Daisaku Ikeda, *Unlocking the Mysteries of Birth and Death: Buddhism in the Contemporary World* (London: Warner Books, 1994), pp. 106-153.

2. *Ibid.*, pp. 114-115; 140-143.

3. *Ibid.*, pp. 128-133.

Chapter Six

1. Daisaku Ikeda, *Unlocking the Mysteries of Birth and Death: Buddhism in the Contemporary World* (London: Warner Books, 1994), p. 33.

2. *Ibid.*

3. *Ibid.*, p. 79.

Chapter Seven

1. Daisaku Ikeda, *Unlocking the Mysteries of Birth and Death: Buddhism in the Contemporary World* (London: Warner Books, 1994), pp. 155-173.

2. René Huyghe and Daisaku Ikeda, *Dawn After Dark*, trans. Richard L. Gage. New York: Weatherhill, 1991), p. 210.

3. Daisaku Ikeda and Arnold Toynbee, *Choose Life: A Dialogue*, ed. Richard L. Gage (Oxford: Oxford University Press, 1976), p. 139.

Chapter Eight

1. Daisaku Ikeda, *Songs from My Heart*, trans. Burton Watson (New York and Tokyo: Weatherhill, 1978), p. 24.

2. Soka Gakkai International-USA. http://www.sgi-usa.net/cgi-bin/lexicon.cgi?exact=on&src=dbtc&term=Kosen-Rufu

3. Ikeda, "Song of Youth," in *Songs from My Heart*, trans. Watson, pp. 21-22.

4. *Ibid.*, 22.

5. Buddha, *The Teaching of Buddha* (Tokyo: Kosaido Printing, Co., 1996), p. 204.

6. Ikeda, "Song of Youth," p. 22.

7. Daisaku Ikeda, *Soka Education: A Buddhist Vision for Teachers, Students and Parents* (Santa Monica, Cal.: Middleway Press, 2001), p. 40.

Chapter Nine

1. Tsunesaburo Makiguchi, as quoted in Dayle M. Bethel, *Makiguchi: The Value Creator* (New York and Tokyo: Weatherhill, 1994), p. 50.

2. Daisaku Ikeda, *Soka Education: A Buddhist Vision for Teachers, Students and Parents* (Santa Monica, Cal.: Middleway Press, 2001), pp. 15-16.

3. Daisaku Ikeda. "The Environmental Problem and Buddhism." *The Journal of Oriental Studies*, 3 (1990), p. 13.

Chapter Eleven

1. René Huyghe and Daisaku Ikeda, *Dawn After Dark*, trans. Richard L. Gage (New York: Weatherhill, 1991), p. 210.

2. Daisaku Ikeda, as quoted in N. Radhakrishnan, *Daisaku Ikeda, The Man and His Mission* (Delhi: National Center for Development Education, 1992), p. 108.

3. Daisaku Ikeda and Arnold Toynbee, *Choose Life: A Dialogue*, ed. Richard L. Gage (Oxford: Oxford University Press, 1976), p. 129.

4. Ikeda, as quoted in Radhakrishnan, *Daisaku Ikeda,* p. 104.

5. Huyghe and Ikeda, *Dawn After Dark*, p. 127.

6. Radhakrishnan, *Daisaku Ikeda,*, p. 107.

7. Daisaku Ikeda, *A Lasting Peace*, Volume 2 (New York and Tokyo: Weatherhill, 1987), p. 83.

Chapter Twelve

1. Daisaku Ikeda, *A New Humanism* (New York and Tokyo: Weatherhill, 1996.), p. 36.

2. *Ibid.*, p. 201

3. Daisaku Ikeda, *A Lasting Peace*, Vol. 2 (New York and Tokyo: Weatherhill, 1987), pp. 32-33.

4. *Ibid.*, p. 259.

5. Daisaku Ikeda, "In the River of Revolution," Ikeda, *Songs from My Heart*, trans. Burton Watson (New York and Tokyo: Weatherhill, 1978.), p. 83.

6. *Ibid.*, p. 84.

7. *Ibid.*

Chapter Thirteen

1. Daisaku Ikeda, *Glass Children and Other Essays* (Tokyo, New York, and San Francisco: Kodansha International LTD., 1979), p. 26.

2. Daisaku Ikeda, *A New Humanism* (New York and Tokyo: Weatherhill, 1996), p. 30.

3. *Ibid.*, p. 55.

4. Daisaku Ikeda, *A Lasting Peace*, Vol. 2 (New York and Tokyo: Weatherhill, 1987), pp. 72-73.

Chapter Fourteen

1. Daisaku Ikeda, *A New Humanism* (New York and Tokyo: Weatherhill, 1996), p. 41.

2. *Ibid.*, p. 42

3. George David Miller, *Negotiating toward Truth: The Extinction of Teachers and Students* (Amsterdam and Atlanta, Ga.: Rodopi, 1998), p. 32.

4. Lao Tzu, *Tao The King*, trans. Archie J. Baum (Albuquerque, N.M.: World Books, 1958, 1986), p. 12.

5. Ikeda, *A New Humanism*, p. 42.

6. *Tao The King*, pp. 25-26.

7. *Ibid.*, p. 26.

8. Regie Gibson, "Alchemy," in *Storms Beneath the Skin* (Joliet, Ill.: EM Press, LLC., 2001), p. 8.

8. George David Miller, "Fluidly Frictional Learning" (Paper delivered in Critical Thinking and Action course, Lewis University, Romeoville, Ill: 6 November 2000).

Chapter Fifteen

1. Daisaku Ikeda and Arnold Toynbee, *Choose Life: A Dialogue*, ed. Richard L. Gage (Oxford: Oxford University Press, 1976), p. 327.

2. Daisaku Ikeda, *A Lasting Peace*, Vol. 2 (New York and Tokyo: Weatherhill, 1987), p. 25.

3. René Huyghe and Daisaku Ikeda, *Dawn After Dark*, trans. Richard L. Gage. New York: Weatherhill, 1991), p. 6.

4. Ikeda and Toynbee, *Choose Life: A Dialogue*, ed. Richard L. Gage (Oxford: Oxford University Press, 1976), p. 334.

5. Ikeda, *A Lasting Peace*, Vol. 2, p. 28.

6. Daisaku Ikeda and Bryan Wilson, *Human Values in a Changing World: A Dialogue on the Social Role of Religion* (Secaucus, N.J.: Lyle Stuart Inc., 1987), p. 271.

7. Daisaku Ikeda. "The Environmental Problem and Buddhism." *The Journal of Oriental Studies,* 3 (1990), p. 13.

8. Daisaku Ikeda, *A New Humanism* (New York and Tokyo: Weatherhill, 1996), pp. 66—67.

Chapter Sixteen

1. Daisaku Ikeda, *A Lasting Peace*, Vol. 2 (New York and Tokyo: Weatherhill, 1987), p. 17.

2. *Ibid.*, 169.

3. Daisaku Ikeda, as quoted in N. Radhakrishnan, *Daisaku Ikeda, The Man and His Mission* (Delhi: National Center for Development Education, 1992), p. 105.

4. René Huyghe and Daisaku Ikeda, *Dawn After Dark*, trans. Richard L. Gage (New York: Weatherhill, 1991), p. 127.

5. Ikeda, *A Lasting Peace*, Vol. 2, p. 207.

6. Daisaku Ikeda and Arnold Toynbee, *Choose Life: A Dialogue*, ed. Richard L. Gage (Oxford: Oxford University Press, 1976), p. 65.

7. *Ibid.*, p. 39

8. *Ibid.*, p. 62

Chapter Seventeen

1. Daisaku Ikeda, *The Cherry Tree*, illustrated by Brian Wildsmith, English version by Geraldine McCaughrean (New York: Alfred A. Knopf, 1991), p. 1

2. Daisaku Ikeda, as quoted in N. Radhakrishnan, *Daisaku Ikeda, The Man and His Mission* (Delhi: National Center for Development Education, 1992), p. 117.

3. Daisaku Ikeda, "Culture and the Great Earth," in *Songs from My Heart*, trans. Burton Watson (New York and Tokyo: Weatherhill, 1978), p. 99.

4. Daisaku Ikeda, *The Way of Youth: Buddhist Common Sense for Handling Life's Questions*, foreword by Duncan Sheik (Santa Monica: CA: Middleway Press, 2000), p. 119.

5. Daisaku Ikeda, *Soka Education: A Buddhist Vision for Teachers, Students and Parents* (Santa Monica, Cal.: Middleway Press, 2001), p. 40.

Chapter Eighteen

1. Plato, *The Republic*, ed. G.R.F. Ferrari, trans. Tom Griffith (New York: Cambridge University Press, 2000).

2. Daisaku Ikeda and Arnold Toynbee, *Choose Life: A Dialogue*, ed. Richard L. Gage (Oxford: Oxford University Press, 1976), p. 349.

3. Daisaku Ikeda, *A Lasting Peace*, Vol. 2 (New York and Tokyo: Weatherhill, 1987), p. 63.

4. *Ibid.*, p. 158.

5. *Ibid.*

6. *Ibid.*, p. 265.

7. René Huyghe and Daisaku Ikeda, *Dawn After Dark*, trans. Richard L. Gage (New York: Weatherhill, 1991), p. 374.

8. *Ibid.*, p. 375.

Chapter Nineteen

1. Daisaku Ikeda, "Song of Youth," in *Songs from My Heart*, trans. Burton Watson (New York and Tokyo: Weatherhill, 1978), p. 16.

2. Daisaku Ikeda, quoted in N. Radhakrishnan, *Daisaku Ikeda, The Man and His Mission* (Delhi: National Center for Development Education, 1992), p. 102.

3. Daisaku Ikeda, *A New Humanism* (New York and Tokyo: Weatherhill, 1996), p. 58.

4. Daisaku Ikeda and Arnold Toynbee, *Choose Life: A Dialogue*, ed. Richard L. Gage (Oxford: Oxford University Press, 1976), p. 318.

5. Daisaku Ikeda, *A Lasting Peace*, Vol. 2 (New York and Tokyo: Weatherhill, 1987), p. 29.

6. *Ibid.*

7. *Ibid.*, 38.

8. *Ibid.*, p. 30.

9. *Ibid.*

10. *Ibid.*, p. 29.

Chapter Twenty

1. Daisaku Ikeda, *A Lasting Peace*, Vol. 2 (New York and Tokyo: Weatherhill, 1987), p. 28.

2. Daisaku Ikeda and Arnold Toynbee, *Choose Life: A Dialogue*, ed. Richard L. Gage (Oxford: Oxford University Press, 1976), p. 25.

3. *Ibid.*, p. 33.

4. René Huyghe and Daisaku Ikeda, *Dawn After Dark*, trans. Richard L. Gage (New York: Weatherhill, 1991), p. 240.

5. Daisaku Ikeda and Bryan Wilson, *Human Values in a Changing World: A Dialogue on the Social Role of Religion* (Secaucus, N.J.: Lyle Stuart Inc., 1987), p. 271.

6. John Polkinghorne, *Quarks, Chaos, and Christianity* (New York: Crossroad, 1996), pp. 11-12.

7. Ikeda and Wilson, *Human Values*, pp. 374-375.

Chapter Twenty-One

1. Lao Tzu, *Tao The King*, 2nd ed., trans. Archie J. Bahm (Albuquerque, N.M.: World Books, 1958, 1986), p. 24.

2. *Ibid.*

3. *Ibid.*

Chapter Twenty-Two

1. Plato, *The Republic*, ed. G.R.F. Ferrari, trans. Tom Griffith (New York: Cambridge University Press, 2000).

Chapter Twenty-Three

1. John Stuart Mill, *Utilitarianism*, ed. with an introduction by George Sher (Indianapolis, Ind.: Hackett Publishing Company, 1979), p. 10.

Chapter Twenty-Four

1. Alfred North Whitehead, *The Aims of Education and Other Essays* (New York: The Free Press, 1929), p. v.

2. *Ibid.*, pp. 6-7.

3. *Ibid.*, pp. 11-12.

Chapter Twenty-Five

1. John Dewey, *Philosophy of Education* (Totowa, N..J.: Littlefield, Adams, & Co., 1958), p. 56.

Chapter Twenty-Six

1. Antonio Gramsci, *Selections from Prison Notebooks*, ed. and trans. Quintin Hoare and Geoffrey Nowell Smith (New York: International Publishers, 1971), p. 9.

Chapter Twenty-Seven

1. Martin Luther King, Jr., *The Strength to Love,* in *A Testament of Hope: The Essential Writings and Speeches of Martin Luther King, Jr.*, ed. James Washington (San Francisco, HarperCollins, 1991), p. 493.

2. *Ibid.*, p. 492

3. *Ibid.*, p. 494.

Chapter Twenty-Eight

1. Paulo Freire, *Pedagogy of the Oppressed*, trans. Myra Bergman Ramos, introduction by Donaldo Macedo (New York: Continuum, 2000), pp. 35-40.

2. *Ibid.*, p. 35.

3. *Ibid.*, p. 72.

4. *Ibid.*, p. 77.

5. *Ibid.*

Chapter Twenty-Nine

1. Howard Gardner, *Multiple Intelligences: The Theory in the Practice* (New York: Basic Books, 1993), pp. 8-12.

2. *Ibid.*, pp. 17-34; http://edweb.gsn.org/edref.mi.th.html

3. Gardner, *Multiple Intelligences*, pp. 72-74.

4. *Ibid.*, p. 244.

Chapter Thirty

1. George David Miller, *Negotiating toward Truth: The Extinction of Teachers and Students* (Amsterdam and Atlanta, Ga.: 1998), pp. 93-143.

Chapter Thirty-One

1. The New Zealand Foundation for Character Education, Inc. http://www.cornerstonevalues. org/education.htlm

2. Madhavi Majmudar. http://www.leeds.ac.uk/educol/documents/000000842.htm

Chapter Thirty-Two

1. Self-Esteem Institute. http://www.theselfesteeminstitute.com/main.html

Chapter Thirty-Three

1. Daisaku Ikeda, *For the Sake of Peace: Seven Paths to Global Harmony; A Buddhist Perspective*, foreword by Glen D. Paige (Santa Monica, Cal.: Middleway Press, 2001), p. 84.

2 *Ibid.*, p. 87.

Chapter Thirty-Four

1. Daisaku Ikeda, *For the Sake of Peace: Seven Paths to Global Harmony; A Buddhist Perspective*, foreword by Glen D. Paige (Santa Monica, Cal.: Middleway Press, 2001), p. 77.

2. *Ibid.*, p. 212.

Chapter Thirty-Five

1. Daisaku Ikeda, *Glass Children and Other Essays*, trans. Burton Watson (Tokyo, New York, and San Francisco: Kodansha International LTD., 1979, 1983), p. 16.

2. Martin Luther King, Jr., *The Strength to Love,* in *A Testament of Hope: The Essential Writings and Speeches of Martin Luther King, Jr.*, ed. James Washington (San Francisco: HarperCollins, 1991), p. 118.

3. Daisaku Ikeda, *For the Sake of Peace: Seven Paths to Global Harmony, A Buddhist Perspective*, Foreword by Glen D. Paige (Santa Monica, Cal.: Middleway Press, 2001), p. 57.

4. Daisaku Ikeda, *Peace through Dialogue: A Time to Talk* (Tokyo, Japan: Soka Gakkai, 2000), p. 14.

5. *Ibid.*

BIBLIOGRAPHY

1. Writings of Daisaku Ikeda

The following represents most of the English translations of Daisaku Ikeda's writings. Soka Gokkai graciously compiled the list for the author.

Advice to Young People. Tokyo: World Tribune Press, 1976.

(and Aurelio Peccei). *Before It Is Too Late*. Tokyo: Kodansha, 1984.

Buddhism and the Cosmos. London: Macdonald, 1985.

Buddhism in Action, Volume I. Tokyo: NSIC, 1984.

Buddhism in Action, Volume II. Tokyo: NSIC, 1985.

Buddhism in Action, Volume III. Tokyo: NSIC, 1988.

Buddhism in Action, Volume IV. Tokyo: NSIC, 1989.

Buddhism in Action, Volume V. Tokyo: NSIC, 1991.

Buddhism in Action, Volume VI. Tokyo: NSIC, 1992.

Buddhism in Action, Volume VII. Tokyo: NSIC, 1993.

Buddhism, the First Millennium. Tokyo: Kodansha, 1982.

Buddhism: The Living Philosophy: Far East Publishing, 1976.

The Cherry Tree. London: Oxford University Press, 1991.

(and Arnold Toynbee). *Choose Life: A Dialogue.* Oxford: Oxford University Press, 1976.

(and Johan Galtung). *Choose Peace*. London: Pluto Press, 1995.

Complete Works, Volume 1. Tokyo: Sokka Gakkai, 1968.

The Creative Family. Tokyo: NSIC, 1992.

Daily Guidance. Los Angeles: World Tribune Press, 1976.

Daily Guidance. Volume 2. Los Angeles: World Tribune Press, 1983.

Daily Guidance. Volume 3. Los Angeles: World Tribune Press, 1986.

(and René Huyghe). *Dawn After Dark*. Tokyo: Weatherhill, 1991.

Dialogue on Life. Volume 1. Tokyo: NSIC, 1976.

Dialogue on Life. Volume 2. Tokyo: NSIC, 1977.

Faith into Action. Santa Monica, Cal.: SGI-USA, 1998.

The Family Revolution. Santa Monica, Cal.: SGI-USA, 1998.

The Flower of Chinese Buddhism. Tokyo: Weatherhill, 1997.

For the Sake of Peace. Santa Monica, Cal.: Middleway Press, 2001.

For Today and Tomorrow: Daily Encouragement. Santa Monica, Cal.: World Tribune Press, 1999.

Glass Children and Other Essays. Tokyo: Kodansha, 1979.

Guidance Memo. Santa Monica, Cal.: World Tribune Press, 1975.

Hopes and Dreams. Santa Monica, Cal.: World Tribune Press, 1976.

The Human Revolution, Volume 1. Tokyo: Weatherhill, 1972.

The Human Revolution, Volume 2. Tokyo: Weatherhill, 1974.

The Human Revolution, Volume 3. Tokyo: Weatherhill, 1976.

The Human Revolution, Volume 4. Tokyo: Weatherhill, 1982.

The Human Revolution, Volume 5. Tokyo: Weatherhill, 1984.

The Human Revolution, Volume 6. Tokyo: Weatherhill, 1999.

(and Bryan Wilson). *Human Values in a Changing World*. London: MacDonald, 1984.

(and Karan Singh). *Humanity at the Crossroads*. New Delhi: Oxford University Press, 1988.

A Lasting Peace, Volume 1. Tokyo: Weatherhill, 1981.

A Lasting Peace, Volume 2. Tokyo: Weatherhill, 1987.

Learning from the Gosho: The Eternal Teachings of Nichiren. Santa Monica, Cal.: SGI-USA, 1997.

(and Yasushi Inoue). *Letters of Four Seasons*. Tokyo: Kodansha, 1981.

Life: An Enigma, A Precious Jewel. Tokyo: Kodansha, 1982.

(and Linus Pauling). *A Lifelong Quest for Peace*. Boston, Jones and Bartlett, 1992.

The Living Buddha. Tokyo: Weatherhill, 1995/

My Dear Friends in America. Santa Monica, Cal.: World Tribune Press, 2000.

My Recollections. Santa Monica, Cal.: World Tribune Press, 1980

The New Human Revolution, Volume 1. Santa Monica, Cal.: SGI-USA, 1995.

The New Human Revolution. Volume 2. Santa Monica, Cal.: SGI-USA, 1995.

The New Human Revolution, Volume 3. Santa Monica, Cal.: SGI-USA, 1996.

The New Human Revolution, Volume 4. Santa Monica, Cal.: SGI-USA, 1996.

The New Human Revolution; Volume 5. Santa Monica, Cal.: SGI-USA, 1997.

The New Human Revolution, Volume 6. Santa Monica, Cal.: SGI-USA, 1998.

A New Humanism: The University Addresses. Tokyo: Weatherhill, 1996.

On the Japanese Classics. Tokyo: Weatherhill, 1979.

Over the Deep Blue Sea. London: Oxford University Press, 1992.

The People. Santa Monica, Cal.: World Tribune Press, 1972.

The Princess and the Moon. London: Oxford University Press, 1992.

(and Josef Derbolav). *Search for a New Humanity*. Tokyo: Weatherhill, 1992.

Selected Lectures on the Gosho, Volume 1. Tokyo: NSIC, 1993.

The Snow Country Prince. London: Oxford University Press, 1990.

Soka Education. Santa Monica, Cal.: Middleway Press, 2001.

Songs for America. Santa Monica, Cal.: World Tribune Press, 2000.

Songs from My Heart. Tokyo: Weatherhill, 1978.

Songs of Victory. Tokyo: NSIC, 1988.

(and Chandra Wickramasinghe). *Space and Eternal Life*. London: Journeyman Press, 1998.

Treasures of the Heart. Tokyo: NSIC, 1998.

Unlocking the Mysteries of Birth and Death. London: Macdonald, 1988.

The Way of Youth. Santa Monica, Cal.: Middleway Press, 2000.

The Wisdom of the Lotus Sutra, Volume 1. Santa Monica, Cal.: World Tribune Press, 2000.

The Wisdom of the Lotrus Sutra, Volume 2. Santa Monica, Cal.: World Tribune Press, 2000.

Yesterday, Today and Tomorrow. Santa Monica, Cal.: World Tribune Press, 1973.

A Youthful Diary. Santa Monica, Cal.: World Tribune Press, 2000.

2. Other Works Cited

Bethel, Dayle. *Makiguchi: The Value Creator*. New York and Tokyo: Weatherhill, 1994.

Freire, Paulo. *Pedagogy of the Oppressed*, trans. Myra Bergman Ramos, introduction by Donaldo Macedo. New York: Continuum, 2000.

Gardner, Howard. *Multiple Intelligences: The Theory in the Practice*. New York: Basic Books, 1993.

Gramsci, Antonio. *Selections from Prison Notebooks*. Ed. and Trans. Quintin Hoare and Geoffrey Nowell Smith. New York: International Publishers, 1971.

King, Jr., Martin Luther. *The Strength to Love,* in *A Testament of Hope: The Essential Writings and Speeches of Martin Luther King, Jr.* Edited by James Washington. San Francisco, HarperCollins, 1991.

Lao Tzu. *Tao The King*. 2nd ed. Translated by Archie J. Bahm. Albuquerque, N.M.: 1958, 1986.

Makiguchi, Tsunesaburo. *Education for Creative Living: Ideas and Proposals of Tsunesaburo Makiguchi*. Trans. Alfred Birnbaum. Ed. by Dayle M. Bethel. Ames, Iowa: Iowa University Press, 1989.

Mill, John Stuart. *Utilitarianism*. Edited with an introduction by George Sher. Indianapolis, Ind.: Hackett Publishing Company, 1979.

Miller, George David. *Negotiating toward Truth: The Extinction of Teachers and Students*. Amsterdam and Atlanta, Ga.: Rodopi, 1998.

Nichiren Daishonin, *Letters of Nichiren*. Trans. by Burton Watson and others. Ed. by Philip B. Yampolsky. New York: Columbia University Press, 1996.

_____. *Selected Writings of Nichiren Daishonin*, ed. with an introduction by Philip Yampolsky. New York and Oxford: Columbia University Press, 1990.

_____. *The Writings of Nichiren Daishonin*, ed. and trans. The Gosho Translation Committee. Tokyo: Soka Gakkai, 1999.

Radhakrishnan, N. *Daisaku Ikeda, The Man and His Mission*. Delhi: National Center for Development Education, 1992.

Whitehead, Alfred North. *The Aims of Education and Other Essays*. New York: The Free Press, 1929.

ABOUT THE AUTHOR

George David Miller teaches philosophy at Lewis University in Romeoville, Illinois and is the author of three other texts in the Value Inquiry Book Series: *An Idiosyncratic Ethics; Or, the Lauramachean Ethics*; *On Education and Values: In Praise of Pariahs and Nomads* (co-authored with Conrad P. Pritscher); and *Negotiating toward Truth: The Extinction of Teachers and Students*. He is co-author of *Global Ethical Options* (Weatherhill) and author of *Children of Kosen-Rufu* (EM Press), his first book of poetry.

Miller has received several teaching awards, including the Carnegie Foundation for the Advancement of Teaching Illinois Professor of the Year in 1997 and the Award of Honor from Soka University of Japan in 2000.

He currently serves as editor of two VIBS special series (Philosophy of Education and Daisaku Ikeda Studies) and co-founded the African American Philosophy special series.

He has served as founding director of the graduate philosophy program at Lewis University and is the founder of the Scholars Academy at the same institution.

APPENDIX: PHOTOGRAPHS

Photograph 2
Josei Toda (standing) and Tsunesaburo Makiguchi around the time of Soka Gakkai's founding (1930)

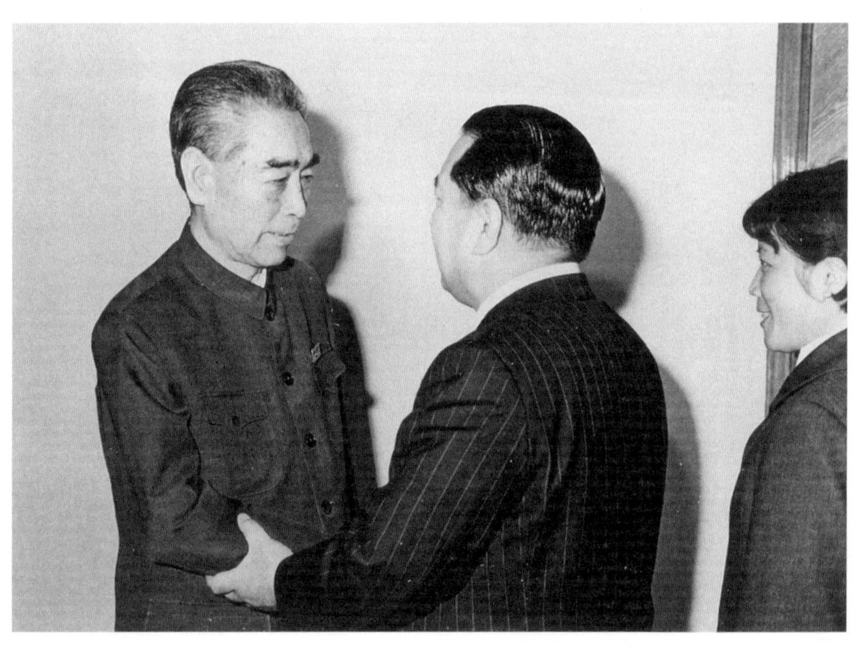

Photograph 3
Daisaku Ikeda (right) meeting with Premier Zhou Enlai of China (December 1974)

Photograph 4
Daisaku Ikeda greeting Nelson Mandela of South Africa (July 1995)

Photograph 5
Daisaku Ikeda with Rosa Parks, pioneer of the American Civil Rights Movement (January 1993)

Photograph 6
Lawrence Edward Carter, Sr., Dean of the Martin Luther King, Jr. International Chapel (right), accompanied by George David Miller (center), inducting Daisaku Ikeda into Martin Luther King, Jr. Collegium of Scholars (September 2000)

Photograph 7
Aerial view of Soka University of America, Aliso Viejo, California (2001)

INDEX

VIBS

The **Value Inquiry Book Series** is co-sponsored by:

Adler School of Professional Psychology
American Indian Philosophy Association
American Maritain Association
American Society for Value Inquiry
Association for Process Philosophy of Education
Canadian Society for Philosophical Practice
Center for Bioethics, University of Turku
Center for International Partnerships, Rochester Institute of Technology
Center for Professional and Applied Ethics, University of North Carolina at Charlotte
Center for Research in Cognitive Science, Autonomous University of Barcelona
Centre for Applied Ethics, Hong Kong Baptist University
Centre for Cultural Research, Aarhus University
Centre for Professional Ethics, University of Central Lancashire
Centre for the Study of Philosophy and Religion, College of Cape Breton
College of Education and Allied Professions, Bowling Green State University
Concerned Philosophers for Peace
Conference of Philosophical Societies
Department of Moral and Social Philosophy, University of Helsinki
Gannon University
Gilson Society
Ikeda University
Institute of Philosophy of the High Council of Scientific Research, Spain
International Academy of Philosophy of the Principality of Liechtenstein
International Center for the Arts, Humanities, and Value Inquiry
International Society for Universal Dialogue

Natural Law Society
Personalist Discussion Group
Philosophical Society of Finland
Philosophy Born of Struggle Association
Philosophy Seminar, University of Mainz
Pragmatism Archive
R.S. Hartman Institute for Formal and Applied Axiology
Research Institute, Lakeridge Health Corporation
Russian Philosophical Society
Society for Iberian and Latin-American Thought
Society for the Philosophic Study of Genocide and the Holocaust
Society for the Philosophy of Sex and Love
Yves R. Simon Institute.

Titles Published

1. Noel Balzer, *The Human Being as a Logical Thinker.*

2. Archie J. Bahm, *Axiology: The Science of Values.*

3. H. P. P. (Hennie) Lötter, *Justice for an Unjust Society.*

4. H. G. Callaway, *Context for Meaning and Analysis: A Critical Study in the Philosophy of Language.*

5. Benjamin S. Llamzon, *A Humane Case for Moral Intuition.*

6. James R. Watson, *Between Auschwitz and Tradition: Postmodern Reflections on the Task of Thinking.* A volume in **Holocaust and Genocide Studies.**

7. Robert S. Hartman, *Freedom to Live: The Robert Hartman Story,* edited by Arthur R. Ellis. A volume in **Hartman Institute Axiology Studies.**

8. Archie J. Bahm, *Ethics: The Science of Oughtness.*

9. George David Miller, *An Idiosyncratic Ethics; Or, the Lauramachean Ethics.*

10. Joseph P. DeMarco, *A Coherence Theory in Ethics.*

11. Frank G. Forrest, *Valuemetrics: The Science of Personal and Professional Ethics.* A volume in **Hartman Institute Axiology Studies.**

12. William Gerber, *The Meaning of Life: Insights of the World's Great Thinkers.*

13. Richard T. Hull, Editor, *A Quarter Century of Value Inquiry: Presidential Addresses of the American Society for Value Inquiry.* A volume in **Histories and Addresses of Philosophical Societies.**

14. William Gerber, *Nuggets of Wisdom from Great Jewish Thinkers: From Biblical Times to the Present.*

15. Sidney Axinn, *The Logic of Hope: Extensions of Kant's View of Religion.*

16. Messay Kebede, *Meaning and Development.*

17. Amihud Gilead, *The Platonic Odyssey: A Philosophical-Literary Inquiry into the* Phaedo.

18. Necip Fikri Alican, *Mill's Principle of Utility: A Defense of John Stuart Mill's Notorious Proof.* A volume in **Universal Justice.**

19. Michael H. Mitias, Editor, *Philosophy and Architecture.*

20. Roger T. Simonds, *Rational Individualism: The Perennial Philosophy of Legal Interpretation.* A volume in **Natural Law Studies.**

21. William Pencak, *The Conflict of Law and Justice in the Icelandic Sagas.*

22. Samuel M. Natale and Brian M. Rothschild, Editors, *Values, Work, Education: The Meanings of Work.*

23. N. Georgopoulos and Michael Heim, Editors, *Being Human in the Ultimate: Studies in the Thought of John M. Anderson.*

24. Robert Wesson and Patricia A. Williams, Editors, *Evolution and Human Values.*

25. Wim J. van der Steen, *Facts, Values, and Methodology: A New Approach to Ethics.*

26. Avi Sagi and Daniel Statman, *Religion and Morality.*

27. Albert William Levi, *The High Road of Humanity: The Seven Ethical Ages of Western Man,* edited by Donald Phillip Verene and Molly Black Verene.

28. Samuel M. Natale and Brian M. Rothschild, Editors, *Work Values: Education, Organization, and Religious Concerns.*

29. Laurence F. Bove and Laura Duhan Kaplan, Editors, *From the Eye of the Storm: Regional Conflicts and the Philosophy of Peace.* A volume in **Philosophy of Peace.**

30. Robin Attfield, *Value, Obligation, and Meta-Ethics.*

31. William Gerber, *The Deepest Questions You Can Ask About God: As Answered by the World's Great Thinkers.*

32. Daniel Statman, *Moral Dilemmas.*

33. Rem B. Edwards, Editor, *Formal Axiology and Its Critics.* A volume in **Hartman Institute Axiology Studies.**

34. George David Miller and Conrad P. Pritscher, *On Education and Values: In Praise of Pariahs and Nomads.* A volume in **Philosophy of Education.**

35. Paul S. Penner, *Altruistic Behavior: An Inquiry into Motivation.*

36. Corbin Fowler, *Morality for Moderns.*

37. Giambattista Vico, *The Art of Rhetoric* (*Institutiones Oratoriae,* 1711-1741), from the definitive Latin text and notes, Italian commentary and introduction by Giuliano Crifò, translated and edited by Giorgio A. Pinton and Arthur W. Shippee. A volume in **Values in Italian Philosophy.**

38. W. H. Werkmeister, *Martin Heidegger on the Way,* edited by Richard T. Hull. A volume in **Werkmeister Studies.**

39. Phillip Stambovsky, *Myth and the Limits of Reason.*

40. Samantha Brennan, Tracy Isaacs, and Michael Milde, Editors, *A Question of Values: New Canadian Perspectives in Ethics and Political Philosophy.*

41. Peter A. Redpath, *Cartesian Nightmare: An Introduction to Transcendental Sophistry.* A volume in **Studies in the History of Western Philosophy.**

42. Clark Butler, *History as the Story of Freedom: Philosophy in Intercultural Context,* with Responses by sixteen scholars.

43. Dennis Rohatyn, *Philosophy History Sophistry.*

44. Leon Shaskolsky Sheleff, *Social Cohesion and Legal Coercion: A Critique of Weber, Durkheim, and Marx.* Afterword by Virginia Black.

45. Alan Soble, Editor, *Sex, Love, and Friendship: Studies of the Society for the Philosophy of Sex and Love, 1977-1992.* A volume in **Histories and Addresses of Philosophical Societies.**

46. Peter A. Redpath, *Wisdom's Odyssey: From Philosophy to Transcendental Sophistry.* A volume in **Studies in the History of Western Philosophy.**

47. Albert A. Anderson, *Universal Justice: A Dialectical Approach.* A volume in **Universal Justice.**

48. Pio Colonnello, *The Philosophy of José Gaos.* Translated from Italian by Peter Cocozzella. Edited by Myra Moss. Introduction by Giovanni Gullace. A volume in **Values in Italian Philosophy.**

49. Laura Duhan Kaplan and Laurence F. Bove, Editors, *Philosophical Perspectives on Power and Domination: Theories and Practices.* A volume in **Philosophy of Peace.**

50. Gregory F. Mellema, *Collective Responsibility.*

51. Josef Seifert, *What Is Life? The Originality, Irreducibility, and Value of Life.* A volume in **Central-European Value Studies.**

52. William Gerber, *Anatomy of What We Value Most.*

53. Armando Molina, *Our Ways: Values and Character,* edited by Rem B. Edwards. A volume in **Hartman Institute Axiology Studies.**

54. Kathleen J. Wininger, *Nietzsche's Reclamation of Philosophy.* A volume in **Central-European Value Studies.**

55. Thomas Magnell, Editor, *Explorations of Value.*

56. HPP (Hennie) Lötter, *Injustice, Violence, and Peace: The Case of South Africa.* A volume in **Philosophy of Peace.**

57. Lennart Nordenfelt, *Talking About Health: A Philosophical Dialogue.* A volume in **Nordic Value Studies.**

58. Jon Mills and Janusz A. Polanowski, *The Ontology of Prejudice.* A volume in **Philosophy and Psychology.**

59. Leena Vilkka, *The Intrinsic Value of Nature.*

60. Palmer Talbutt, Jr., *Rough Dialectics: Sorokin's Philosophy of Value,* with Contributions by Lawrence T. Nichols and Pitirim A. Sorokin.

61. C. L. Sheng, *A Utilitarian General Theory of Value.*

62. George David Miller, *Negotiating Toward Truth: The Extinction of Teachers and Students.* Epilogue by Mark Roelof Eleveld. A volume in **Philosophy of Education.**

63. William Gerber, *Love, Poetry, and Immortality: Luminous Insights of the World's Great Thinkers.*

64. Dane R. Gordon, Editor, *Philosophy in Post-Communist Europe.* A volume in **Post-Communist European Thought.**

65. Dane R. Gordon and Józef Niznik, Editors, *Criticism and Defense of Rationality in Contemporary Philosophy.* A volume in **Post-Communist European Thought.**

66. John R. Shook, *Pragmatism: An Annotated Bibliography, 1898-1940.* With Contributions by E. Paul Colella, Lesley Friedman, Frank X. Ryan, and Ignas K. Skrupskelis.

67. Lansana Keita, *The Human Project and the Temptations of Science.*

68. Michael M. Kazanjian, *Phenomenology and Education: Cosmology, Co-Being, and Core Curriculum.* A volume in **Philosophy of Education.**

69. James W. Vice, *The Reopening of the American Mind: On Skepticism and Constitutionalism.*

70. Sarah Bishop Merrill, *Defining Personhood: Toward the Ethics of Quality in Clinical Care.*

71. Dane R. Gordon, *Philosophy and Vision.*

72. Alan Milchman and Alan Rosenberg, Editors, *Postmodernism and the Holocaust.* A volume in **Holocaust and Genocide Studies.**

73. Peter A. Redpath, *Masquerade of the Dream Walkers: Prophetic Theology from the Cartesians to Hegel.* A volume in **Studies in the History of Western Philosophy.**

74. Malcolm D. Evans, *Whitehead and Philosophy of Education: The Seamless Coat of Learning.* A volume in **Philosophy of Education.**

75. Warren E. Steinkraus, *Taking Religious Claims Seriously: A Philosophy of Religion,* edited by Michael H. Mitias. A volume in **Universal Justice.**

76. Thomas Magnell, Editor, *Values and Education.*

77. Kenneth A. Bryson, *Persons and Immortality.* A volume in **Natural Law Studies.**

78. Steven V. Hicks, *International Law and the Possibility of a Just World Order: An Essay on Hegel's Universalism.* A volume in **Universal Justice.**

79. E. F. Kaelin, *Texts on Texts and Textuality: A Phenomenology of Literary Art,* edited by Ellen J. Burns.

80. Amihud Gilead, *Saving Possibilities: A Study in Philosophical Psychology.* A volume in **Philosophy and Psychology.**

81. André Mineau, *The Making of the Holocaust: Ideology and Ethics in the Systems Perspective.* A volume in **Holocaust and Genocide Studies.**

82. Howard P. Kainz, *Politically Incorrect Dialogues: Topics Not Discussed in Polite Circles.*

83. Veikko Launis, Juhani Pietarinen, and Juha Räikkä, Editors, *Genes and Morality: New Essays.* A volume in **Nordic Value Studies.**

84. Steven Schroeder, *The Metaphysics of Cooperation: The Case of F. D. Maurice.*

85. Caroline Joan ("Kay") S. Picart, *Thomas Mann and Friedrich Nietzsche: Eroticism, Death, Music, and Laughter.* A volume in **Central-European Value Studies.**

86. G. John M. Abbarno, Editor, *The Ethics of Homelessness: Philosophical Perspectives.*

87. James Giles, Editor, *French Existentialism: Consciousness, Ethics, and Relations with Others.* A volume in **Nordic Value Studies.**

88. Deane Curtin and Robert Litke, Editors, *Institutional Violence.* A volume in **Philosophy of Peace.**

89. Yuval Lurie, *Cultural Beings: Reading the Philosophers of* Genesis.

90. Sandra A. Wawrytko, Editor, *The Problem of Evil: An Intercultural Exploration.* A volume in **Philosophy and Psychology.**

91. Gary J. Acquaviva, *Values, Violence, and Our Future.* A volume in **Hartman Institute Axiology Studies.**

92. Michael R. Rhodes, *Coercion: A Nonevaluative Approach.*

93. Jacques Kriel, *Matter, Mind, and Medicine: Transforming the Clinical Method.*

94. Haim Gordon, *Dwelling Poetically: Educational Challenges in Heidegger's Thinking on Poetry.* A volume in **Philosophy of Education.**

95. Ludwig Grünberg, *The Mystery of Values: Studies in Axiology,* edited by Cornelia Grünberg and Laura Grünberg.

96. Gerhold K. Becker, Editor, *The Moral Status of Persons: Perspectives on Bioethics.* A volume in **Studies in Applied Ethics.**

97. Roxanne Claire Farrar, *Sartrean Dialectics: A Method for Critical Discourse on Aesthetic Experience.*

98. Ugo Spirito, *Memoirs of the Twentieth Century.* Translated from Italian and edited by Anthony G. Costantini. A volume in **Values in Italian Philosophy.**

99. Steven Schroeder, *Between Freedom and Necessity: An Essay on the Place of Value.*

100. Foster N. Walker, *Enjoyment and the Activity of Mind: Dialogues on Whitehead and Education.* A volume in **Philosophy of Education.**

101. Avi Sagi, *Kierkegaard, Religion, and Existence: The Voyage of the Self.* Translated from Hebrew by Batya Stein.

102. Bennie R. Crockett, Jr., Editor, *Addresses of the Mississippi Philosophical Association.* A volume in **Histories and Addresses of Philosophical Societies.**

103. Paul van Dijk, *Anthropology in the Age of Technology: The Philosophical Contribution of Günther Anders.*

104. Giambattista Vico, *Universal Right.* Translated from Latin and edited by Giorgio Pinton and Margaret Diehl. A volume in **Values in Italian Philosophy.**

105. Judith Presler and Sally J. Scholz, Editors, *Peacemaking: Lessons from the Past, Visions for the Future.* A volume in **Philosophy of Peace.**

106. Dennis Bonnette, *Origin of the Human Species.* A volume in **Studies in the History of Western Philosophy.**

107. Phyllis Chiasson, *Peirce's Pragmatism: The Design for Thinking.* A volume in **Studies in Pragmatism and Values.**

108. Dan Stone, Editor, *Theoretical Interpretations of the Holocaust.* A volume in **Holocaust and Genocide Studies.**

109. Raymond Angelo Belliotti, *What Is the Meaning of Human Life?*

110. Lennart Nordenfelt, *Health, Science, and Ordinary Language,* with Contributions by George Khushf and K. W. M. Fulford.

111. Daryl Koehn, *Local Insights, Global Ethics for Business.* A volume in **Studies in Applied Ethics.**

112. Matti Häyry and Tuija Takala, Editors, *The Future of Value Inquiry.* A volume in **Nordic Value Studies.**

113. Conrad P. Pritscher, *Quantum Learning: Beyond Duality.*

114. Thomas M. Dicken and Rem B. Edwards, *Dialogues on Values and Centers of Value: Old Friends, New Thoughts.* A volume in **Hartman Institute Axiology Studies.**

115. Rem B. Edwards, *What Caused the Big Bang?* A volume in **Philosophy and Religion.**

116. Jon Mills, Editor, *A Pedagogy of Becoming.* A volume in **Philosophy of Education.**

117. Robert T. Radford, *Cicero: A Study in the Origins of Republican Philosophy.* A volume in **Studies in the History of Western Philosophy.**

118. Arleen L. F. Salles and María Julia Bertomeu, Editors, *Bioethics: Latin American Perspectives.* A volume in **Philosophy in Latin America.**

119. Nicola Abbagnano, *The Human Project: The Year 2000,* with an Interview by Guiseppe Grieco. Translated from Italian by Bruno Martini and Nino Langiulli. Edited with an Introduction by Nino Langiulli. A volume in **Studies in the History of Western Philosophy.**

120. Daniel M. Haybron, Editor, *Earth's Abominations: Philosophical Studies of Evil.* A volume in **Personalist Studies.**

121. Anna T. Challenger, *Philosophy and Art in Gurdjieff's* Beelzebub: *A Modern Sufi Odyssey.*

122. George David Miller, *Peace, Value, and Wisdom: The Educational Philosophy of Daisaku Ikeda.* A volume in **Daisaku Ikeda Studies.**